DEDICATION

First, to my daughter Hailey, who provided the title for the book. Astounding me yet again with her brilliance.

Second, to all the men of ODA 1114, who had forced upon them the unenviable task of teaching a grown man how to be a team player.

Contents

Introduction

"All humans are entrepreneurs not because they should start companies but because the will to create is encoded in human DNA."

— Reid Hoffman, LinkedIn co-founder

* *

Your father, Kaidu, ruler Changatai Khanate, is Grandson of Ogedei, great-grandson of Genghis and cousin and rival of Kublai, who's both Khan and Yuan Emperor. Your father will become the most powerful ruler Central Asia has ever known, extending his rule from Mongolia to the Oxus and from Central Siberian Plateau to India. Youngest of your father's 15 children, you're unquestionably his favorite. With 10,000 horse herd, some say you won as wagers from defeated suitors, you'll train and lead one of the fiercest heavy cavalry regiments in history. Cavalry you'll use again and again, assisting your father in many battles during 30-years of war. You're your father's most trusted advisor and political supporter.

Great-great-granddaughter of incomparable Genghis Khan. A Princess. In your own time and in your own right, you're recognized as skilled and experienced warrior and leader, proof of Mongol views on women. Mongol women holding seats in the Kurulurai, managing conquered cities while men fought, building public works, dispensing justice, managing largest land empire the world has ever known. At times, even fighting in battles beside your men.

Marco Polo, Rashid al-Din and the Yuan, all chronicle your exploits and extol your strength as superb warrior, powerful wrestler and skilled politician and general. Marco Polo described you as a cool and courageous warrior. Writing, you would ride up to the enemy, grab their leader and bring him back to your father before turning to strike with your cavalry. Your skills are so great, before his death in 1301, your father will try to make you his successor, Katun. But as youngest and only girl, you instead support claim of your brother Orus on condition you lead his armies. You're Khutulun (1260–1306), one of the most powerful women humanity has ever produced. Your wit, sheer strength, and brilliant leadership echo throughout the ages.

****

We're now living in what is only the third reorganization of humanity to ever occur over course of past several million years. First was transition from nomadic hunter-gathering organizational models to those of agrarian, roughly 11,000 years ago. Second was transition from agrarian to industrial organization fostered by the industrial revolution, beginning roughly 250 years ago. This third great reorganization we're experiencing now as you read this book, is transition from industrial to postindustrial organization. As with the first two transitions, everything is changing, absolutely everything. Not in small ways, but fundamentally. What is changing specifically and most profoundly is how individual humans contribute to the social and economic groupings they belong to and how and to what degree they are compensated for these contributions.

Civilization is quite literally evolving at pace and scale never before imagined in all the long past of human history. Here we are, before even getting our feet fully under us from last great reorganization. Yet another civilization-wide upheaval.

This is no small matter. It's critical we understand this near absolute change is irreversible. With related uncertainty root cause for why we find it so incredibly difficult anymore, if not nigh on to impossible, to know where and how to apply ourselves. Difficulty arising from fact, all our many known and familiar systems, processes and organizations are being cannibalized. Shifts and changes are taking place in every domain of human existence. Inconceivable changes not witnessed nor possible to predict, even after massive shifts of the first two cataclysmic reorganizations. Changes we've yet to fully grasp and most likely won't for another century or more. Most immediate and impactful of these changes of course, is to our individual and collective place and value in civilization.

While there are many complimentary and competing forces arising from this rapid and wholesale evolution. To get a grasp on how we might best contribute upon further targeted self-development. We need to recognize three of these forces are by far most important to adapt ourselves to. Specifically, in the context of our own current and future economic and societal contributions:

-        First is rapidly ever-deepening interconnectedness and complexity of absolutely everything

-        Second is the ever-greater impermanence of systems, processes and organizations

-        Third, arising from the first two, is increasing role of short-lived high-functional teams

These three forces, incredibly powerful independently, when combined, become colossal. In ways we're only beginning to understand despite all our best efforts. These three forces are so vastly powerful they require an incredibly broad and fundamental rewrite of how we think of and how we develop ourselves. In particular, to be considered an expert, we must now develop subject matter expertise across more than one domain or field. While at the same time, making of ourselves, quite productive members of highly functional teams.

In a world where everything is becoming more complex, intricate and integrated, where everything is changing at an ever-faster pace. Where our computers are rapidly becoming better defined field specialists than humans ever could. In this new world, being subject matter expert of a domain or even a field, is no longer sufficient. Unpleasant truth is, the postindustrial era is rushing to a place where humans are less and less necessary for what we must consider to be industrial era expertise and labour, both physical and intellectual. What remains for this postindustrial era will be those things which smart machines, AI-enhanced machines, can't do. At least, can't do for some decades or a century or more yet to come.

Having spent the last thirty-eight years of my life engaged in some form or fashion in research, design, development and application of a broad array of technologies. The past four years in particular, conducting research in the interrelated domains of machine learning and artificial and augmented intelligence, this around PhD studies in Interdisciplinary Engineering, emphasizing Computational Engineering. I can attest unabashedly, there's yet necessity for the human, for unique capacities of the human brain and mind. Specifically, the human brain's ability to recognize and grasp the nuanced and counterintuitive interconnections between things. Not merely the ever more intricate and complex 'how' machines are beginning to outpace us in. But rather, all critical, 'what' and 'why'. What's its purpose, what does it contribute, what part does it play in the far greater whole, what are reaching ramifications of its succeeding or failing, and why this and not something else, why should we care and participate, why is this of value to humanity and not only the bottom line?

In virtually every single failure I've been a part of or have witnessed or read of. Was failure to answer these questions led to that failure. With many of these failures, negatively impacting the lives of those directly involved, entire communities, ecosystems and even society as a whole. While simple appearing, these are ever-harder questions to answer. Rising complexity and connectedness of everything means every one of these questions is now a constantly changing, multivariant, multidimensional problem. With answer, not possible from individual leader or domain expert. Instead, requiring a high-functional team of skilled and seasoned experts. Increasingly, a short-lived and highly focused team purpose assembled for only this specific task, answering these questions in a specific context, getting this whatever out there into the marketplace rapidly. Given this, there's yet a place for the human. A place for those who, can assemble or be a contributing member of a team of highly skilled individuals. A team of individuals with the required diversity of backgrounds, skills, abilities, relationships and all the necessaries to plot a course of action and attain a specific goal quickly. This before the team being dissembled, with individuals moving on to their next team.

Effective teamwork was an incredible struggle to attain and maintain during the industrial era, with far less complexity than today and where virtually everything was reduceable to defined specialties. Standardized and replaceable cogs in the great machine. Where well-functioning organizations ran on ever more specialized roles, staffed by combinations of domain specific experts. Attaining effective teamwork in the postindustrial era is proving to be orders of magnitude more difficult. As we depend more and more upon high-functional teams populated by skilled generalists. Problem is, we've not produced capable broad-spectrum generalists for at least two centuries. A gap we're not overcoming, as experts for the most part continue to attempt solutions based on industrial management and discredited postmodernist social theories. Making transition from industrial era models of business and institutional organization and management to postindustrial era models requires we step outside the norm, the known and accepted, as these all rapidly recede behind us.

We don't need to scrap everything and start from scratch. Much like with any great transition in anything. Much of the old is required of the new, however, requiring evolution into new forms and models the old system, its organizations and best practices are incapable of adapting. Not only incapable of adapting, but by their very nature, disincentivized to do so. So, where do these new forms and models come from, it being impossible to create anything from nothing? Turns out, to our great fortune, we do stand on the shoulders of giants. Most what is needed exists. There's always form and model revisioning going on. This from innovators and innovative ways of thinking. Last Mile thinkers, out there beyond the frontier of the well-established, creating order out of chaos. Knee-deep in very harsh uncertain reality of it all, working collaboratively in high-functional teams, finding solutions to truly hard problems. Adapting the old to the new, most often in highly counterintuitive ways, plucking success when the only option is that or destruction, annihilation or both.

While not claiming to be an expert in these matters, or any matters at all really, half a century of life has blessed me to be a member of many different teams, across broad spectrum of endeavours. In many different environments, from the well-established corporate and banking world, to the uncertain world of startups and startup investing and to the world of immensely high Risk and Uncertainty of Special Forces and combat. Been on effective teams, solid teams, ineffectual teams, even utterly horrible teams. This last, rather rare occurrence, as truly horrible teams make up only a tiny fraction of those we experience in life. Most probably because they tend to be short-lived. Like all of us, I've been on many different types of teams also, and in many different domains. Sports, academia, science, technology, startups and corporations, banking and finance and other domains. Having been involved in tech design and development, business and financial analysis and operations, investment due diligence, modeling and funding, academic research, combat, Special Operations and so much more. Like you, most often, involved with more than one team concurrently. Honestly, for me at least. Not a bit of it has been easy.

As with so many others, team player isn't something comes naturally to me, given my own psychological constitution is rather introverted and reclusive. In early 2000's however I was forced to accept, were I to progress in career and life, take responsibility for making contributions seriously. I'd have to learn to become a successful, regularly contributing member of high-functional teams. Since roughly 2003, this has been a major topic of my study, thoughts and sought out experiences. In 2009, it was a good part of why I chose to leave a successful career in tech startup investing and investment banking to join Special Forces. This in order to force myself into becoming a team player, against all my inherent cognitive biases to contrary. Accepting the possibly impossible task ahead of me, early 2009, I set to learning from and working with the undisputed masters of the Human

Domain, the social domain, teamwork and team life. From those who've for seventy years now been outside the Core and Edge, out beyond the frontier, in the chaos of the Last Mile of humanity, creating order out of sheer chaos. All the while facing the very real threat of destruction and even annihilation. That is, learning from and with, US Army Special Forces, the Green Berets. To up necessity to get it right, force myself to change. I joined in a time of war. Being further honest, can't say my years of forced neural rewiring were easy on my teammates and SF colleagues. For that I here apologize. To some of you, the good teammates.

Just to reiterate, I'm no expert. But with two decades in and around technology startups in Silicon Valley and China and a decade in Special Forces, two domains with extensive similarities I've written about for some years. Having been involved in one way or another with hundreds and hundreds of teams of highly capable individuals, across an incredible array of domains, all over the world, under virtually every circumstance imaginable. There are a handful of concepts I've distilled out to help me better contribute as a team player. Concepts related to where we are in this great reorganization of humanity, why getting teams and teamwork right matters. Concepts related to teams themselves and how we develop them. The concepts detailed in this book, are for those in or joining hypercompetitive and hyperpaced world of startups. The world of suddenly and rapidly changing high-functional teams.

As with Special Forces and more broadly Special Operations, in startups, requirement for being a successful member of a high-functional team is, well, not to overstate the matter, EVERYTHING. Much like the Operational Detachment Alpha of the Green Berets, unlike corporations and large institutions, startups are less organizations than they are purpose assembled teams composed of broadly skilled and proven generalists. No fail teams, with absolute requirement each generalist contributes maximally as integrated member. Around requirements and in conditions constantly changing, requiring each member of the team also constantly evolve, change and adapt. Requiring each individual be prepared at a moment's notice to join yet another team, accomplish yet another impossible task, adapt themselves to yet another set of skills and capacities, to yet another group of unique individuals. All impossible without firmly understanding the forces at play within ourselves, and how interplay between these forces plays out, in and across groups and groupings.

Over course of three decades academic and professional life, I've come to accept. High-functional teams require constant balancing between competing forces within the individual, team and across teams and organizations. Across ecosystems and economies, which are complex webs of high-functional teams of teams. Over the years, I've distilled out a 5 Vector Model provides understanding of the powerful competing forces we individually and collectively contend with and constantly balance. I've also come, reluctantly, to accept. Malevolence is real and prevalent among us. While not one of the 5 Vectors, it is riddled through absolutely everything we face, confront and do, every moment of every day. Without an understanding of very real malevolence, we can get everything else right, be contributing high-functional team members. And yet fail. Everything we've done, undone through the unmitigated malevolence of others.

May you find something of value in this, for your own journey to becoming a team player, or better team player.

Postindustrial Economy

"The secret to successful hiring is this: look for the people who want to change the world."

— Marc Benioff, Salesforce CEO

****

Born in Norfolk, Virginia, 1840. It's believed you escaped via the Underground Railroad, joining your father then in New England. When the Civil War breaks out, you'll join as a sergeant, having taught yourself to read and write. Serving with 54th Massachusetts Volunteer Infantry. In 1863, at the assault on Fort Wagner, South Carolina. You'll pick up the flag after the Color Guard is killed. You'll press forward to plant the  flag on the parapet. And, despite multiple severe wounds, you'll continue even as Union troops are being beaten back. Under fire the entire way, you'll struggle back across the battlefield, before handing the colors to another survivor. A year later you'll be discharged from service due to injuries sustained that day, never once having let flag touch the ground.

May 1900, 37 years after your heroics. You'll finally receive your country and the US Military's highest honor, the Congressional Medal of Honor. Twenty other African Americans received theirs before you, but your actions on the battlefield came before all theirs, making you the first black man in history to earn the CMoH. You're William H. Carney (1840-1908), slave become soldier, become tireless civil servant and mentor in your community. Through your actions on the battlefield and the life dedicated to quiet contribution you lived after, you'll forever be recognized as a truly great individual, man and role model for all.

Your citation reads:

> When the color sergeant was shot down, this soldier grasped the flag, led the way to the parapet, and planted the colors thereon. When the troops fell back he brought off the flag, under a fierce fire in which he was twice severely wounded.

****

It's not only nature of work, roles, titles, responsibilities and compensation changing ever more rapidly in unpredictable ways. Irreversible demographic shifts, vastly more powerful than economic trends, greatest driver of economic trends, are more so shaping the postindustrial world. The three greatest demographic and thereby economic trends, reshaping the world, concurrent to transition to postindustrial era, are:

-    Decline in traditional Western populations, in and from Europe, North America, New Zealand and Australia. | With population replacement rates below sustainable levels for more than forty years. Even were everyone of European descent to start having five kids per family. Would take more than 100 years to restore traditional European populations;

-    State sponsored immigration into the Western nations, Europe, North America, New Zealand and Australia. | Compensating for decline in traditional populations, needing to sustain economies, ensure sufficient rents for landlords, sales for corporations, debtors for lenders, dependents for non-profits, politicians and government agencies. Western powers are increasingly relying upon what is in effect, forced immigration.

-     Return of historical locus of power from Europe and North America to Asia, particularly, the Far East where the greatest power and wealth resided for vast part of human history. | With more than 60% of the world's population, highly advanced economies in Japan and South Korea, rising economic and political power in China, increasing economic might in India and rise of ASEAN. Asia is beginning to dominate this Century.

What the first two mean, is at same time critical importance of high-functional teams is becoming dominate reality. The very nature of these teams is changing in ways never before experienced. Not only in the nature of skills and multiskilled individuals needing to populate them, not only in nature of what these teams are spun up to accomplish, not only in the transient nature of these teams. Ever more so these teams and their members, contest with non-homogeneous populations, with members from vastly different cultural, socio-economic, linguistic, educational and other related backgrounds. Which only increases complexity, making collaboration orders of magnitude more difficult.

Despite increased difficulties, multiculturalism and diversity are here to stay. Even if only in the West. Not because they inherently improve everything as we're being forced to believe. No credible study conducted by any credible, unbiased researcher in any business or any other professional environment, has ever demonstrated multiculturalism and diversity to miraculously improve things. Quite the contrary. Both have been shown in numerous studies, to substantially increase input requirements, this while both lowering quality and timeliness of outcomes. Often being stated as root cause for why individuals of what's spun up to be a high-functional team, fail to adhere together and go on to accomplish the task successfully. This despite each member being of the highest caliber, with the right education, skills and experience for the purpose of the team.

Multiculturalism and diversity are here to stay, this due to irreversible demographic and resultant political and socio-economic shifts. Again, in the West only, as nowhere else in the world are populations being forced to merge as they are in the West. So, we better figure out how to make it all work. To be clear, when it comes to high-functional teams, doesn't mean there isn't real merit and value in multiculturalism and diversity, because there is. Diversity of thought arising from different backgrounds and experiences, can add substantially. But it's just that, diversity of thought. Not unintentioned thought, but highly developed, tested and proven thought with valiance to the whole, neither imaginary nor merely for a subset thereof. Thought with valance doesn't arise simply because one is of a different gender, ethnic, educational or socio-economic background. It arises because the individual, irrespective of these things, put in the years of hard work to be of value to the team and mission. All the many different teams and missions they'll be a part of in course of their life.

What third great trend means, with respect to high-functional teams, is that the way we assigned value increasingly since the Enlightenment, is being challenged. Reigniting the most ancient of civilizational conflicts. One single difference in thought, stirring East and West to near countless number of wars spanning more than forty centuries. Western thought holding value is resident more within the individual than the whole. Eastern thought holding value is resident more within the whole than the individual. Small, yet incredibly profound difference in beliefs, making it nearly impossible for those who grow up in one belief system, to find compatibility with the other. Because, at the neurological level, those who grow up in the East and those grow up in the West, literally are hardwired to value things differently.

It's impossible in a single tome, much less one of this brevity, to go into any real detail as to the ramifications of the legions of changes occurring as we inexorably, grudgingly, perhaps a bit disconcertingly, move into the postindustrial world. Nor is it possible to detail the exact right courses of action. This, as the postindustrial era, unlike the industrial era, is one of incredibly high degrees of probability with ever less absolute certainty. Leaving the heavy lifting, that of detailing what the postindustrial world is becoming, to the academics and professionals, who for most part, will contemplate, articulate and get wrong for several decades. Will herein focus on high level concepts and models for high-functional teams. Concepts and models constantly being adapted and proven today, in the very real world, both within and beyond the frontier of first world communities. Teams composed of broadly skilled generalists, with highly diverse backgrounds and experiences and from a vast array of cultures. Testing, adapting and practicing high-functional teamwork out in the world's many zero-fail environments, outside safety and comforts of corporate HR departments, and Ivory Towers of academia and professional consulting.

Before moving on to discuss why US Army Special Forces, the Green Berets, are the very model of and for postindustrial high-functional teams. Before discussing some concepts and models derived from their more than seventy years of "on the ground" tested and proven experience. Need first discuss in brief three further increasingly widespread trends gaining power and strength as we make transition from industrial to postindustrial globally interconnected economy. Intertwined forces Green Berets mostly, though certainly not alone, are paying the price for, on the ground out there every day in 185 nations in war or open conflict. Directly confronting the forces fueling conflict and war to a degree never before seen in all human history, not even during two World Wars and all of the Cold War. As context, in 185 of only 195 nations.

- Identity Politics – Modern Tribalism | Since beginnings of time, from that of our ancestors, primates on the plains of Africa, through to today. Individuals have ascertained their value through their own productivity contributions. Contributions in the form of Labour, both physical and intellectual and in the form of invested Capital. As our increasingly globalized economy relies less and less on human inputs, as Capital pools in the hands of a smaller and smaller number of individuals and families. What vast majority of humanity is left with, by which to know personal value, is Identity Politics and contributions to the defense of their tribe(s). As we slide deeper into this economic system transition. Identity Politics is spreading, while evolving into that historically most destructive and deadly of forces, Tribalism. Tribalism, very antithesis of multiculturalism and diversity, as the inescapable end-state of Identity Politics.

- Zero-Sum – Non-Zero-Sum | Deeply embedded within and conflating Identity Politics wars. Is another conflict arising from a simple but fundamental difference in how brains are physically wired. Conflict between far larger percentage wired for zero-sum thinking and far smaller percentage wired for non-zero-sum thinking. The former believing given we only have limited resources, gains for one group must inevitably come at the loss to another. The latter believing resources are finite, but we'll devise better optimization solutions, such gains for one need not come at expense of another. This difference in thinking, introduces untold amounts of conflict into our lives and communities, even in times when there are manageable levels of Tribalism. This, due to Zero-sum thinkers believing they must compete for absolutely everything. Making things even more difficult, there's another fundamental difference in the two brain types. Zero-sum thinkers believing optimal solutions exists for everything, Non-Zero-Sum thinkers believing there's no such thing as a universally optimal, solution. As we transition, there are powerful Zero-Sum thinkers, having attained ever greater degrees of power during the regimented and certain world of the Industrial Era. Out there in our communities, fueling Identity Politics and Tribalism, fostering wars and conflicts, including right here in our own comfortable first world communities. All so they may retain and add to their power.

-   Philanthropy – Modern Colonialism | Believing our civilization has a limited amount of resources. Believing poverty is root cause of Identity Politics and Tribalism, of rising tensions and animus. Believing corruption and criminality are the reason why communities can't break the poverty cycle. Believing there are untold numbers of humans exist can't do for themselves. The first world has set about the task of creating a vast and powerful global welfare state. Trillions of dollars ostensibly focused on riding the world of poverty, disease and corruption. As Vikram Seth wrote in *A Suitable Boy*, "God save us from people who mean well." While laudable. Around the world, these efforts are seen by an ever-greater number of people and communities as Modern Colonialism. The First world creating a globalized industry, the Poverty Industry. Already by far the world's largest industry. A vast ecosystem all to its own. Far reaching and powerful dependency system touching every corner of the world. A system patterned on the first world's own dependent communities, leaving hundreds of millions looking forward to little real change, to futures of crime, violence and multigenerational dependency. It's dependency fed resentment, product of a lack of or perceived lack of upward mobility, reason Identity Politics and Tribalism are growing, creating fertile ground for Zero-Sum thinkers to initiate and sustain conflicts and wars.

This point you're asking yourself what any of this has to do with high-functional teams and startups. Three things. First, all these forces and dynamics are ceaselessly playing out, not only at the level of communities, societies and civilization, but also within each of us, between individuals, within and between teams, organizations, institutions. Second, as teams become more diverse, populated by individuals from many communities, cultures and backgrounds, it's critical to understand how and why each sees the world as they do. And third, to provide context for why concepts and models developed for the ODA "Operational Detachment Alpha" of the US Army Special Forces, purpose designed to address these very dynamics and forces, are best for high-functional team assembly, development, evolution and operation, in the postindustrial era and transition to.

Since early 2009, spent considerable time researching and practicing Irregular and Unconventional Warfare, with a bit of General Warfare thrown in. This to better understand how Special Operations Forces could benefit from Silicon Valley startups and startup investing models and practices. This to improve Stability Operation efforts around the world. Also, to attain and translate for startups, lessons learned becoming a team player, as part of an ODA, for a short time on a Task Force managing deployed ODAs, then again on a specialty ODA conducting counterterrorism and counterproliferation. For a decade now, I've written extensively on the value of SOF supporting local entrepreneurship, employing Silicon Valley like the Venture Capital mind to realize real returns. And I've thought out and written on how to apply Special Forces derived team and teamwork models to startups.

Following are a sampling of these articles on Special Forces and startups, adapted to the intent of this book and enhanced by two new works, on the 5-Vector Model and Malevolence.

Operational Detachment Alpha

"When you walk in silence your excellence will always speak for you."

— Onyi Anyado, Entrepreneur, Author, Speaker

****

Born in Lindenau, Texas, son of Mexican American father and Yaqui Native American mother. At two, your father will die of tuberculosis, five years later your mother will die of same. After, you and your eight cousins will be raised by your uncle, aunt and grandfather. You'll work as a shoeshine, farm labourer and at a tire shop, dropping out of school at age 15 to support your family, to this point having only attended  school sporadically. 1952, during the Korean War, you'll enlist in the military. 1959, you'll be assigned to 82nd Airborne Division, before completing Special Forces qualification and being assigned to 5th Special Forces Group, Studies and Observations Group.

1965, you'll arrive in South Vietnam as advisor to the Army of the Republic of Vietnam. During a patrol you'll step on a landmine. Angered by anti-American sentiment at home, despite being told you'd never walk again, you begin unsanctioned nightly training ritual, crawling to wall, forcing your broken body to work again. After a full year of hospitalization, you walk out of the hospital. 1968, five months after returning to Vietnam, hearing over the radio a 12-man ODA team was surrounded by a North Vietnamese infantry battalion of 10,000. You'll board a helicopter moving to supply and extract the trapped ODA, armed only with knife and medical bag. Under intense fire, you'll jump from the helicopter and move to begin treating the wounded. You'll receive seven gunshot 28 fragmentation wounds, both arms will be slashed by bayonets. You'll have fragments in head, scalp, shoulder, buttocks, feet, and legs. Your right lung will be destroyed. You'll incur injuries to mouth and back of the head. An AK-47 bullet will have entered your back, exiting just beneath your heart. Thought dead, you'll be put into a body bag, to be pronounced dead once more once your body is returned to base camp. **Body bag being zipped up, you spit in the doctor's face, letting him know you're alive.**

You're Raul Perez "Roy" Benavidez, MSG SF(ret) (1935–1998), the poor, poorly educated, orphaned son of Mexican and Native American descent. For your actions that day, during "6 Hours in Hell", you'll one day receive this nation's highest military honor, the CMoH. Deeply driven to improve the lives of the downtrodden and oppressed, you'll go on and become of the most respected warriors in history, speaker, author and strong proponent of kids staying in and finishing school. You were and are to this very day, an inspiration to all the generations after you.

Your Citation reads:

> Master Sergeant (then Staff Sergeant) Roy P. Benavidez United States Army, who distinguished himself by a series of daring and extremely valorous actions on 2 May 1968 while assigned to Detachment B56, 5th Special Forces Group (Airborne), 1st Special Forces, Republic of Vietnam. On the morning of 2 May 1968, a 12-man Special Forces Reconnaissance Team was inserted by helicopters in a dense jungle area west of Loc Ninh, Vietnam to gather intelligence information about confirmed large-scale enemy activity. This area was controlled and routinely patrolled by the North Vietnamese Army. After a short period of time on the ground, the team met heavy enemy resistance, and requested emergency extraction. Three helicopters attempted extraction, but were unable to land due to intense enemy small arms and anti-aircraft fire. Sergeant Benavidez was at the Forward Operating Base in Loc Ninh monitoring the operation by radio when these helicopters returned to off-load wounded crewmembers and to assess aircraft damage. Sergeant Benavidez voluntarily boarded a

returning aircraft to assist in another extraction attempt. Realizing that all the team members were either dead or wounded and unable to move to the pickup zone, he directed the aircraft to a nearby clearing where he jumped from the hovering helicopter, and ran approximately 75 meters under withering small arms fire to the crippled team. Prior to reaching the team's position he was wounded in his right leg, face, and head. Despite these painful injuries, he took charge, repositioning the team members and directing their fire to facilitate the landing of an extraction aircraft, and the loading of wounded and dead team members. He then threw smoke canisters to direct the aircraft to the team's position. Despite his severe wounds and under intense enemy fire, he carried and dragged half of the wounded team members to the awaiting aircraft. He then provided protective fire by running alongside the aircraft as it moved to pick up the remaining team members. As the enemy's fire intensified, he hurried to recover the body and classified documents on the dead team leader. When he reached the leader's body, Sergeant Benavidez was severely wounded by small arms fire in the abdomen and grenade fragments in his back. At nearly the same moment, the aircraft pilot was mortally wounded, and his helicopter crashed. Although in extremely critical condition due to his multiple wounds, Sergeant Benavidez secured the classified documents and made his way back to the wreckage, where he aided the wounded out of the overturned aircraft, and gathered the stunned survivors into a defensive perimeter. Under increasing enemy automatic weapons and grenade fire, he moved around the perimeter distributing water and ammunition to his weary men, re-instilling in them a will to live and fight. Facing a buildup of enemy opposition with a beleaguered team, Sergeant Benavidez mustered his strength, began calling in tactical air strikes and directed the fire from supporting gunships to suppress the enemy's fire and so permit another extraction attempt. He was wounded again in his thigh by small arms fire while administering first aid to a wounded team member just before another extraction helicopter was able to land. His indomitable spirit kept him going as he began to ferry his comrades to the craft. On his second trip with the wounded, he was clubbed from behind by an enemy soldier. In the ensuing hand-to-hand combat, he sustained additional wounds to his head and arms before killing his adversary. He then continued under devastating fire to carry the wounded to the helicopter. Upon reaching the aircraft, he spotted and killed two enemy soldiers who were rushing the craft from an angle that prevented the aircraft door gunner from firing upon them. With little strength remaining, he made one last trip to the perimeter to ensure that all classified material had been collected or destroyed, and to bring in the remaining wounded. Only then, in extremely serious condition from numerous wounds and loss of blood, did he allow himself to be pulled into the extraction aircraft. Sergeant Benavidez' gallant choice to join voluntarily his comrades who were in critical straits, to expose himself constantly to withering enemy fire, and his refusal to be stopped despite numerous severe wounds, saved the lives of at least eight men. His fearless personal leadership, tenacious devotion to duty, and extremely valorous actions in the face of overwhelming odds were in keeping with the highest traditions of the military service, and reflect the utmost credit on him and the United States Army

* *

Given the dearth of experience and background so prevalent among first time founders and co-founders. Reducing Risk, realizing all critical ROI for shareholders and stakeholders, which is dependent on solid planning and decision making. Necessitates startup teams operate as high-functional teams from even before the very first day of operation. This is true for high-functional teams coming together to work on any involved problem, collaborating, succeeding in the rapidly changing, ever more probabilistic everyday business world. Vastly more so in the ultra-competitive, ultra-high Risk and Uncertainty world of startups. Meaning, those on investor side the table must be exceedingly careful with respect to the teams they invest in. Careful thought given to leadership and the team as a functioning whole. The requirement to invest in the entire team rather than only leadership, founders and co-founders, leads to an overarching principle. Invest in the team rather than the idea. Both are important. But, no matter how solid idea or market upside, things change and if the team can't recognize, rapidly adapt and deliver, they fail.

Being successful in the world of early-stage startup investing, really in any and all team-dependent efforts at creating assets, improving asset values, in environments of ultra-high-Risk and Uncertainty. Very much including the Irregular Warfare of Special Forces. Requires modeling and assigning a value, financial value, at different points in time, this more so to the team or teams composed of uniquely skilled and experienced professionals, as the early-stage venture and its assets are of far smaller value. Modeling tangible and intangible assets, heavily emphasizing the later. Despite all the many valuation tools, concepts and models created for the purpose, very few investors, managers, executives or HR departments ever get this right. With more than 75% of all startups, out of the less than 10% receive any funding at all, and 85% of corporate initiatives, failing to realize required ROI. Special Forces, however, due to very nature of what it does. Doesn't have the luxury of anything even remotely close to these failure rates. Actually, neither do postindustrial era individuals working on teams spun up for limited duration to address a very specific need. Increasingly, as is the case with Special Forces. Develop a reputation for not contributing, being a disruption, or more generally, for joining teams that fail to realize ROI. You'll find it difficult to get many offers to join a high-functional team in the on-demand labor market of the postindustrial economy.

Over the course of seven decades, SF, in order to always be as close to zero fail as is humanly possible, while remaining broadly and rapidly adaptable to on the ground truth, without reducing ultra-high functionality. Invests massive resources, energy and time to evolve and real-world "market" test, best methods, practices and procedures for assessing, developing, employing and realizing quantifiable returns from tangible and intangible assets. All this emphasizing the individual as substantial contributing member of a high-functional team, the Operational Detachment Alpha. Contributing, in spite of environment, circumstances, team composition, resources, external supports or any other considerations impact mission success or failure. This operating as part of a multicultural and diverse team of skilled individuals from every walk of life around the world, educated and overly educated alike, from the very poor to the very wealthy. Living, working, conducting ultra-high-Risk operations, often out beyond the frontier of the security bubble of first world communities, on the ground, surrounded by hostile intent. Confronted by the very real world, not the illusionary world of Hollywood, academia, HR departments and Politicians, where the world, as artificial construct, is whatever their feelings or agenda will allow. Regardless what the on the ground truth may be. GBs are right now as you read this, all over the world, successfully operating as contributing member of their high-functional team, creating and improving asset values, in the actual world. The world of startups and Special Operations alike, where reality is constant conflict, Risk and Uncertainty, not giving a damn about your feelings or agenda.

Important to provide here, brief overlay of the mission of the Green Berets. This, so the reader isn't inclined to dismiss the ODA as merely another military entity, with no real valance to the private sector, specifically, to startups and startup investing. And let's be honest, virtually no military entity or related practice or procedure, despite all the many books and business leadership course to the contrary, has. We'll begin with the Seven Elements of National power, otherwise known as the DIMEFIL: Diplomacy; Information; Military; Economics; Finance; Intelligence and Law Enforcement. 1952, at the inception of Special Forces, members becoming known as Green Berets in 1961, SF was tasked with conduct of the first four elements, or the DIME mission. Specifically, in context of advising and assisting oppressed peoples so they would be well-versed and practiced in good governance, security and economics. This to free and govern themselves, having established fully functioning nation states in the true Westphalian model.

While formally tasked with the DIME mission, in practice, conducting countless missions around the world for more than 70 years. Special Forces has found Green Berets must be conversant across all the DIMEFIL, prepared to apply complex combinations of each and all in order to realize ROI. Accepting that while the M "Military" is critical, on its own, it provides zero ROI. This is not to say that while it's the other elements realize the ROI, that they can do so without the M. History's proven, they can't. The first I "Information", is of such importance, SF was spun out of then Psychological Operations. The E & F "Economics" and "Finance" have proven to be central requirements, such a doctrine around Money as a Weapon System has been devised, tested and adopted, leading to Civil Affairs in modern incarnation. The L "Law Enforcement" has gained substantial importance in this age of terrorism, with terrorist organizations and entities, transnational gangs and bad state actors integrating together into powerful global criminal enterprises. In practice what this means, is each GB must be conversant in every aspect of nation states, alliances and conflicts between nation states. Everything from diplomacy to broad spectrum information attainment and analysis, all things military, economics and finance and everything intelligence and law enforcement related. Very same any quality startup leadership team and their investor should be versant in, as impacts success of the startup and their investment.

This means, despite having been battlefield proven as among the world's uncontestably deadliest fighters, Green Berets must first and foremost be experts of the Human Domain and teachers. Known as diplomat warriors in many circles, Green Berets are purpose trained and practiced in Population-centric Warfare, which is shaping the Human Domain. Only

1% of which is combat related. Shaping the Human Domain requiring thorough understanding of the many nuanced combinations and ways in which to apply the 7-Elements, to influence populations and key leaders, including enemies, to come together, design, developed and work collaboratively on common purpose and goals. Often under attack from all sides and within. Not only must the Green Beret operate as contributing member of their own high-functional team, everywhere in the world, at every level of civilization, from dirt streets and mud huts of poor communities to the very halls of power of first world nations. They must also know how to value and develop local peoples, so these peoples go on to improve their own individual and collective value. Becoming themselves contributing members of their own high-functional teams. This at level of small groups, armies, economic ecosystems and up through to the level of nation states and the alliances between.

The Special Forces Operational Detachment Alpha of the US Army, fully self-contained twelve-man element, is designed modularly in order to adapt to rapid changes in environment and need. Members of an ODA, Green Berets, are capable of operating as 12-man, 6- man and 3-man teams, even at times as a 1-man singleton, with each sized element still self-contained and fully operational. Regardless the environment, conditions, need or threat level. This made possible by the very high degree of cross training between Green Berets on the many specialties, roles and responsibilities each member is personally trained in and tasked with. Also, much like with a startup, this is possible because each member is ready and is often called upon to step in and fill any need at any time, even if well outside their specific role and function. More so however, ODAs are so incredibly capable as high-functional teams, regardless configuration. Due to the fact each GB is versed in diplomacy, leadership, staffing, training, combat, logistics, medicine, communications, engineering and all the many more required domains, at least a year and a half in the schoolhouse before getting to a team, attending many more schools through a career. Reason for all this preparation and continued education, is every GB is prepared, starting 1st day of SF training, to individually command an element as large as a battalion, 600 individuals or more, at a moment's notice, under any circumstances and conditions, anywhere in the world. True even of youngest and newest members of the Regiment, fresh out of the Q Course. Not only prepared to conduct war, but more so to build up local peoples to go on and establish their own functional nations and everything required of just such.

This isn't to say Green Berets and ODA are interchangeable, suited to any mission or tasking required. Quite the contrary. Regional specialization begins in the Qualification Course with language and cultural studies. Once GB arrives at their SF Company, they'll then find themselves assigned to a team further specialized as to unique skillsets or capabilities it is responsible for. The GB will also be assigned with skills and duties additional to their Military Occupational Specialty, requiring further schooling and which they'll need maintain as subject matter expert for team, and in some cases, for the Company and Battalion. The combinations can and do get staggering when looking at the hundreds and hundreds of skillsets necessary to meet a wide array of needs in targeted areas in every corner and community of the world. Not to mention when adding in incredible mixture of professional experiences each GB incurs in the course of their service, which makes each one even more unique. Much like startup teams, composed of individuals with diverse backgrounds, some already having been in one or more startup, in one or more domain, filling one or more role and responsibility.

As with startup investors, when an SF commander is assessing which team to invest in, give a specific mission to.

They must take into account and value a considerable number of tangibles and intangibles. The process quality SF commanders take is much like due diligence process of startup investors. With greater emphasis on valuing the intangibles. Intangibles such as:

• Personality of the team, and does this match with the partner force, Country Team and whomever may be in higher command (Are the startup leaders a good social fit for the personality of market percipients; investors, partners, allies and key customers);

• Operational tempo of the ODA which both exhausts and destroys families leading to troops not being in the fight mentally (While they may be highly capable, will the startup team leaders and members have the energy and focus to get to ROI);

• Whether the mission enhances the skills, capabilities and reputation of the team, company and battalion leading to greater capacity (With all critical valuation improvement being based more on good-will than hard asset value, is this best choice to increase good-will);

• Does the mission address real or perceived needs, and who is determining that need and what is their intent (Does the market really need/want this and will they pay for it now, or is this a vanity project around something you care about); And

• Should the personnel, resources and capacities of the team be applied elsewhere or in another fashion to meet a more urgent need (While all of the above may be yes, is this startup founding team better suited to realizing near-term ROI pivoting to something other than planned).

Alright. Enough about what ODAs and Green Berets are, how their organized, trained and employed, heavy emphasis on high-functional teams, and the many similarities they have with startups. Let's get to the good stuff. Principles we can apply in our own lives as startup leaders and contributing members of high-functional teams. The best starting point is the principle of Running Gun Battles. Something we all live with and experience in our own personal and professional lives. Seemingly the thing we all deal with, very thing life is about for all of us, regardless our backgrounds or capacities. Before moving on to the next chapter and a discussion of what a Running Gun Battle is and how to get through them successfully.

Running Gun Battles

"Don't be afraid to assert yourself, have confidence in your abilities and don't let the bastards get you down."

— Michael Bloomberg, Bloomberg L.P. founder

****

Born to the Chihenne band of Apache, sister to a prominent chief. After your womanhood ceremony you let it be known you'll never marry. Instead you request the Council allow you to undertake Hardship of Dikohe, warrior training. Proving to be fierce with war club and accurate with spear, bow and rifle, you'll go on to ride and fight with the men. Your brother, Victorio, will say you are, "…my right hand, strong as a man, braver than most, and cunning in strategy…shield to her people." In 1877, after betrayal on part of the US Government, you'll leave the reservation with your brother, marauding and raiding while evading capture by the military.

At the Rio Grande, hotly pursued by US Cavalry, you turned your horse into the raging river, rifle high above your head. Infusing courage into the women and children too afraid to enter and cross the river. Then you turn back to join the warriors fighting and delaying the enemy as your people safely cross. Despite being your brother's strategist, you'll leave his side to escort a mother and her newborn through Mexican and American held territory. Unable to use your rifle, as sound would bring the enemy, you stalk, kill and butcher a longhorn with only a knife. Followed by stealing a Mexican Cavalry horse and escaping with the young mother and child under a hail of gunfire. You'll steal a vaquero's horse and a soldier's saddle, rifle, ammunition, blanket, canteen and shirt. Before getting young mother and her child safely to the reservation.

Learning of Victorio's death, along with majority of his warriors, you wend your way through enemy patrols joining survivors and fighting beside 74-year-old patriarch, Nana. You'll join and fight beside Geronimo in last Apache Wars in 1885, before leaving the battlefield to lead peace treaty negotiations. You're Lozen (1840-1889), guerilla warfare expert, female warrior, strategist, seer and prophet of Chihenne Chiricahua Apache. Your bravery, cunning, strength and loyalty to your people will never be forgotten.

* *

Before moving on to Running Gun Battles and Irregular and Unconventional Warfare derived team related concepts. To provide small bit of context for how life, particularly startup life, is like a sequence of Gun Battles. Just a few reluctantly attained truths collected over half a century of life, having led and invested in startups, served on an ODA, as a father, academic and technologist, and generally just in the pursuit of life's many other endeavours. Concepts refined in combat and these years of contemplation have come after. This before proceeding to the more usable, how you can use any of this in pursuit of your own path to greater success as a team player in your startup.

-       Life's a competitive team sport, a lifelong series of fights taken up together as a collaborative effort. Though there are a few championship events along the way, ultimate, decisive victory is an impossibility;

-       While we can only develop our personal self, there's not a single accomplishment in life isn't the result of a team effort. This makes improving self into a quality team player, everything;

-       Won't be a single team in our life capable of taking on every fight that we'll have to enjoin. This means we have to adapt ourselves constantly to new teams and fights;

-       Most difficult thing we'll ever do, is train our minds and psyche to remain fully committed and competitive, while not seeking victory in every fight. It's about winning the greatest percentage of fights across the entirety of a life, not about winning any single fight;

-       We must pick our teams with careful deliberation. Only joining those teams whose fight at this moment is a fight moving us to our own next higher level of competition. Making certain also, at least one teammate is highly seasoned in this particular type of competition;

-       Love of Self, Pursuit of Happiness, Political Correctness, Identity Politics, Tribalism and all the Blank Slate lies, nearly stripped us of ability to fight and defend ourselves. Never forget, we don't compete for any of these, fighting instead for the meaning only found taking responsibility for living a life of contribution to the many teams we will be blessed to join.

Something Dwight Eisenhower once stated has always been in my mind over the many years coming to these truths:

"When you are in any contest, you should work as if there were - to the very last minute - a chance to lose it. This is battle, this is politics, this is anything."

Given the truths immediately above, everything prior, this admonition from President Eisenhower, I believe we can now discuss startups and Running Gun Battles. RGBs – not to be confused with RPGs – being:

1. an argument continues over a long period of time;

2. a fight takes place as one group chases another.

Business is total war, infinite combinations of competitions, even more so when conducting the Unconventional Warfare of very early-stage startups. A war composed of many RGBs, at times fought independently, concurrently and overlapping. Each RGB itself a sequence of interrelated competitions, single events, fights. These single event fights affectionately known as firefights. While the objective for the overall war is to seek to win, getting to a place of mutual benefit equating to best possible outcome for all involved, most often what winning is. The objective of an RGB on the other hand is to gain an advantage leading to success along one or more lines of effort in the far greater war: marketing, staffing, legal, product development, logistics, market positioning, and the list goes on. In each firefight however, nested within one or more RGB, the objective is simply to prevail intact, being ready to move on to the next firefight, which can and will occur at any moment.

For clarity, in the context of startups, let's further define the two forms of competition contained in the definitions of an RGB. That is, forms of competition flare up into a firefight of either the "argument" (conflict) or "fight" (combat) type altercation. These being.

1- *Argument*: reason or set of reasons given with the aim of persuading others that an action or idea is right or wrong;

2-   *Fight*: vigorous struggle or campaign for or against something.

With respect to teams, and our activities as members of. We should conceptualize the first, *argument*, as conversational competition, a firm or heated dialogue leading to a given set of ideas being adopted. We should conceptualize the second, *fight*, as actional competition, deliberate actions taken such a given set of ideas dominates. Of course, there's a bit of one within the other. With fights virtually always arising from arguments, over misunderstandings, offense or the standard everyday difference of opinion. Fights often only available recourse to persuasive but erroneous or fallacious arguments. Fights being required as response to forceful external threats. Far more rare, as fight ensues, arising from the chaos if it, an argument will be found allows those involved to back down from the fight. Though this invariably leads only to further argument, that can and will flare at any moment back into a fight.

Millenia old, hard earned wisdom is that: wars are never won; peace is only a break in the hostilities; and, no battle ever decides the war. Business is a never-ending cycle of fights and arguments spawning one another, over and over again. Conflicts and combat quite literally going on for months and years, with a vast number of firefights occurring throughout. Hence applicability of the concept of RGBs. Particularly the RGBs of the Unconventional Warfare of startups and Special Forces. Where your team is behind enemy lines, outgunned, out resourced, developing and improving assets all the while ceaselessly threatened and under attack. With everything so tenuous a single firefight can actually, unlike the general warfare of established corporations, represent a catastrophic event. RGBs being contests over prolonged periods of time, which are not the war itself, but represent some critical effort within. RGBSs being a running series of individual firefights arising from moment to moment needs to drive the purpose of the RGB and greater war forward to some form of success. Only real difference in a given firefight being, whether of the *argument* or *fight* type, the weapons used in the first are mostly words, while those in the second are mostly actions.

As with the war itself, the sole purpose of which is to attain, hold and grow market share. No RGB is ever actually won. They merely evolve over time, at the rate of change, driving it, being driven by it. Shaped and guided by the many nested firefights within. Most of these firefights small and almost unobservable, often a conflict of wills more than a force of arms. What this means is that while there'll be great battles you and your startup team must prepare for and take on. Success in one or all of these will provide little more than a temporary break in the hostilities. Even great wars, leading to such things as success in the wild for startup Unicorns, are composed of nothing more than interrelated RGBs and the many firefights taken on daily by individuals, working alone or in small groups, who prevail in many single engagements. Given this, while we must understand the RGBs we're a part of, where they fit in the greater war, this in order to shape our thinking and efforts. We must also ensure we develop ourselves such we prevail in an individual, often one-on-one, firefight. Even more so, as Carl Jung admonished, we should "embrace our shadow," so we may enjoy and thereby thrive in a firefight. As the saying goes, "there was a firefight and it was glorious!"

That inevitably firefights will spring up anywhere, anytime, between anyone, over anything and everything, particularly in the uber-competitive and ultra-high-Risk and Uncertainty environments of Special Forces and startups. That you must prevail in these firefights, even if not having walked away with a definitive win. Necessitates setting aside sentiment, emotion-laden decision-making, self-delusion and the 250^+ known cognitive biases, which all lead to unnecessary fights. Or worse, to our being undone in a firefight by someone not weakened, bound and restricted by such things. Being undone at times by ourselves, as we most certainly have our own internal gunfights (quick thought specific one-on-one shootout), our internal firefights made up of these gunfights and our own RGBs and the war they make up. This last being our life's contributions and work.

Given all of this, there're five principles which apply to all RGBs, to all firefights and the gunfights they are composed of, whether individually or as a team, whether engaged with others or only our own unperfected self. Equally applicable on and off the battlefield:

1- *Bring a Gun you're proficient with* – You can't prevail if not armed with a weapon, if not as well-prepared, capable and willing to use it as your opponent is theirs. More importantly, in critical moments of necessity as the firefight ensues, you can't prevail if you don't stand your ground and shoot back;

2- *Incoming rounds have the right of way* – Doesn't matter what your intentions, plans and strategy are, nor how you and others perceive you. All are irrelevant when you're pinned down and taking incoming fire. When in a firefight, only thing matters is suppressing enemy fire, such you can survive and go on to fight again;

3- Make haste but do so slowly – The longer rounds are flying through the air. Greater the probability random chance will turn against you. Same time, rushing too fast represents equal danger in the fact you can't know what you don't know and that thing you don't know can destroy you in an instant;

4-   *It's not over till they can't shoot back* – Don't think for a second you've won because rounds aren't currently whizzing around you, striking your body armour. Unless you know for as fact, they can no longer shoot at you. Assume they're reloading, awaiting reinforcements or maneuvering to an improved position from which to defeat you; and

5-   *You're shooting to save others* – When caught in a firefight, neither you nor your opponent matters. Only one's matter are your teammates and those innocents who'll be harmed if you fail. While you may be the immediate target, you're merely first step in your opponent's strategy. If you don't hold the line and prevail, they'll next attack others, including your teammates and those others who can't defend themselves without your guns in the fight, holding the line.

Here in the Western world, where for generations now we've sought to convince ourselves of the lie that competition is a negative human trait, a lingering remnant of a primitive past. Competition as an undesirable thing we can just magically evolve beyond, simply by wishing it so. This despite more than thirty years of research, evidence and science to the contrary. In this world, where we've been taught to never stand our ground, never shoot back and prevail in a firefight. In this illusionary world we cling to, where conflicts, fights and those few who do stand up for themselves and others, are vilified and shunned. Lest we be forced to face the truth of the world as it is, of our own frailty and need to harden so as we may prevail in life's inevitable firefights and Running Gun Battles. In this now far more dangerous world we've inadvertently allowed, there should be a sixth and overriding principle:

-    Get the F%$# out of the line of fire – If you simply can't rise to the challenge of being in a firefight, whether of the conflict or combat type, of actively participating in life's many RGBs. Then get behind something solid and stay out of the way, or you'll get someone killed. Most likely the one risking it all to protect you.

Over the decades since becoming interested in the subject as a child, I've spent a considerable amount of time researching and contemplating social species, wolves, chimps, gorillas, dolphins and others. All to get a grasp on why our progress through life, personally and professionally, is a ceaseless moving between Running Gun Battles. With success in life coming at the expense of joining, surviving and prevailing in firefights. What I've come to accept, is while we should like to think we've becoming something more than evolution has designed us to be. We have in fact not. Nor can we. And perhaps, nor should we. Competition for resources, for mates, for the propagation of our genes runs deep in all of us, even those who don't believe they're competitive.

This competition composed of RGBs and their firefights, is first an internal process, with the many modules of the brain competing for dominance in our decision-making processes. A never-ending competition between our near endless array of hope, want, feeling, desire, resentment, everything that flits through our mind in a day. All fueling and fueled by the environment we find ourselves in. All organized into a matrix of interrelated RGBs, with competition internal to and between each and all. The brain runs on firefights.

Balancing 5-Vectors

"Any person seasoned with a just sense of the imperfections of natural reason, will fly to revealed truth with the greatest avidity."

— David Hume, Philosopher

****

Born into privilege, you draw upon elite education and reputation as a military hero to run for Congress in '46 and for the Senate in '52. 1960, age of 43, you're elected 35th president of United States, then its youngest and first Catholic president. Driven strongly by belief in capacity within all individuals, you lead drive for public service and will sign into law the Peace Corps while providing federal support for growing civil rights movement. During your term as president, you'll also confront mounting global Cold War tensions in Cuba, Vietnam and elsewhere.

Veteran of World War II, leading proponent of unconventional warfare and soft power, you recognize shift to population-centered guerilla warfare, the critical importance of small team operations over large military activities. In speech to Congress you state, "They possess...a well-trained underground in nearly every country, the power to conscript talent and manpower for any purpose, the capacity for quick decisions, a closed society without dissent or free information, and long experience in the techniques of violence and subversion...they prey on unstable or unpopular governments, unsealed, or unknown boundaries, unfilled hopes, convulsive change, massive poverty, illiteracy, unrest and frustration."

You're John F. Kennedy (1917-1963) and your assassination in Dallas will send shockwaves around the world, changing you from all-too-human man into larger-than-life figure. Your support of Civil Rights and Unconventional Warfare and strength in face of Soviet aggression, would set course for the future of humanity. To this day you're revered by Baby Boomers and U.S. Army Green Berets alike, while historians place you in ranks of best-loved presidents in American history.

****

Our cognitive and emotive existence. Basically, everything we think feel and do. Seem to arise from unrelenting warfare between a limited number of competing master cognitive processes. Processes drive ceaseless movement back and forth along their own internally coded vectors, continuums. Vectors composed of conflict between two highly relational yet diametrically opposed aspects of being, one at each extreme. With gain in one aspect invariably at expense of the other. Each movement along continuum between extremes, centering only momentarily on a specific aspect, transitory decision made, acted upon. Generally, with ninety percent or more of this done without any conscious thought at all. This while each cognitive process itself, competes ruthlessly with the other four master cognitive processes for our very limited neurological resources.

Evolution, across hundreds of millions of years, hardwired all this relentless conflict right into the physical brain. Into our neurological and neuropsychological brains and minds.

Structures and processes which underly and drive the more than 250 known cognitive biases hard coded in. Not only is this conflict hardwired into the overall brain and emergent mind. The left and right hemispheres code these master cognitive processes for the exact same vectors, but with values along each continuum assessed differently. Left coded for certainty, employs static values derived from historic knows. Right coded for context, employs ever fluctuating values derived from best current approximations. Not only does each Master Cognitive Process "MCP" vie for dominance, not only does each hemisphere and its different MCP valuations vie for dominance. But each of the vast array of neurological and neuropsychological modules within the brain and mind also relentlessly and ruthlessly compete for dominance. Never ending and ruthless, total war of balancing between interests.

While this holds true within our own brains and lives. Same never-ending conflict resolved balancing, plays itself out between individuals, teams, organizations, corporations, ecosystems, industries, governments and nations. All human groupings, all the way up through civilizations and across historical time frames. Seems despite all our many scientific and technological advances. Biology, neurology more precisely, yet dominates every aspect of our existence, our every thought and action. With most of it going completely unrecognized by anyone unseasoned in meditative practices. Truth is. It's lucky we survive sane at all. Sanity due, quite fortunately, to evolution having also built in controls. That is, MCPs themselves acting as controls which work to ensure this competition in the brain doesn't get too out of hand.

Vectors embedded within five MCPs, at least, as distilled out in my own research and meditative practice. Relate directly to these controls. Controls designed by evolutionary processes and hardwired in over hundreds of millions of years. Built into brain structures at molecular level, into electromotive potentials at the electrical level and into cognition/psychometry at the neuropsychological level. Controls, operating at all three levels simultaneously, within each hemisphere and all three brains, as Master Cognitive Processes.

Each MCP, driven by an embedded Vector, break roughly into the following:

Processing – **Social** | Regarding status within groups

Vector – *Introversion | Extroversion*

Seeks to understand Things ↔ Seeks to understand People;

Processing – **Cognitive** | Regarding information analysis

Vector – *Probabilistic | Deterministic*

Models for Uncertainty ↔ Models for Certainty;

Processing – **Motivation** | Regarding intentioned focus

Vector – *Mission | Rules*

Emphasizes Mission ↔ Emphasizes Process;

Processing – **Reward** | Regarding what is valued

Vector – *Life | Career*

Prefers Life Experiences ↔ Prefers Labour Contributions;

Processing – **Hierarchy** | Regarding leadership style

<u>Vector – *Alpha | A-Type*</u>

Relying on Influence ↔ Relying on Authority.

You might be asking at this point, so, what does all this have to do with teams and being a team player. Well, quite simply, it's impossible to be a solidly contributing team member if we don't understand and have control over ourselves. That's, both internally and externally, when we're alone or in the company of others, as well as when at rest, engaged in work or an outright firefight. Attaining this control is not a simple task, given not a one of us is unidimensional. We're each and all of us multidimensional both neuropsychologically and neurocognitively, with major fluctuations in each throughout the day and across days. Fluctuations taking place along all vectors simultaneously or at different rates and in different directions. Trying to get a grasp on it, most of us attempt to reduce complexity down to a single dimension, I am or they are, this or that kind of person, or in this or that kind of mood. Gross oversimplifications leading to the far greater part of human conflict and combat, to include actual wars.

We're multidimensional, even the boring and tedious among us. Not only are we all multidimensional but what we are at the neurological level is constantly changing throughout the day and across days. This due to fact our brains and minds are constantly taking input, processing and acting upon this processed information, which itself creates even more input to process and act upon. Driving a vast degree of movement back and forth along each Vector. These 5-Vectors, primary forces, movements back and forth along them between the two extremes they model for. These are our own internal RGBs, with firefights of thought and emotion fluctuations, impacted by and driving movement back and forth along the

Vector organic to each RGB. The complexity of it all quickly becomes staggering. I spent two years of my PhD studies in Computational Engineering looking at this very problem. How to model the individual in order to improve prediction as to behaviour. Though this work in context of multivariant sentiment analysis related specifically to investing. Before coming to this more feasible 5-Vector Model, there were 20 Vectors. Which proved, even with robust physics software written in Fortran, to be computationally far too burdensome.

What I found in those years of study and after, more recently in neuropsychology studies related to brain injury detection and treatment. Is that while we perceive we're dealing with a near infinite number of emotions and thoughts. In reality, all these are only variations, arising from movements along the vectors of primary RGBs, those of the 5-Vector Model. Think light and how its immense variations arising simply from movements back and forth across wavelength spectrum, from ultraviolet to infrared. Using this 5-Vector Model enables us to substantially reduce the variables and their near infinite combinations necessary to arrive at a rather thorough understanding of ourselves at any given moment. Instead of all the infinite ways in which we can and do interpret our thoughts and feelings, generally incorrectly, we can narrow this process down to only a handful of values. As example:

-      *5 Vector Balance*: This morning I'm a bit withdrawn (Social | reclusive) thinking about all the things I don't know (Cognitive | probabilistic) about the new market segment we're preparing to move into (Motivation | mission) which, if successful will result in a promotion (Reward | career). I'm also not looking forward to the detailed report I have to give my micromanaging and difficult boss Thursday (Hierarchy – A-Type).

- *Simple Rebalance*: Spend the morning or day working at home or in the office with door closed, conducting research and analysis on the new market segment. Prepare first draft of the report ensuring the content is detailed and touches on all the data points and strategy questions this boss needs to look good to their boss.

- *5-Vector Balance*: Today, my legal team lead for this project is spending a lot of time talking with everyone about the company event (Social | extraversion). We have a response to a request for information from the SEC regarding specific rules (Motivation | rules) which she knows best (Cognition | Deterministic). She's leaving early today to spend time with her son before he goes off to college (Reward | life). As she doesn't respond well to the direct approach, I'm going to have to find an indirect way to influence her to focus on the deliverable (Hierarchy | alpha)

- *Simple Rebalance*: Legal team lead is very responsive to her staff, mentoring and coaching. Will have her paralegal ask for guidance on base document language, around specific questions. Then have paralegal follow up within a couple hours with request to review key sections of document language derived from response to initial questions. Will first however catch my legal team lead when she's in her office. Let her know how much I don't want to keep her in the office and away from her son on his last day at home.

- *5-Vector Balance*: We've team of highly specialized software engineers who keep to themselves (Social | introverted), focusing all their time to highly detailed coding necessary to be within banking compliance (Cognition |

deterministic). They're rushing work to make deadlines and their code is beginning to show errors representing possible security risks to our firm (Motivation | mission). Our annual review is coming up and everyone's working hard to complete tasks, get a bonus (Reward | career). Their manager, one of only a small handful of subject matter experts in these systems and compliance, has done everything he can, but team isn't responding to coaching and mentoring efforts (Hierarchy | alpha).

- *Simple Rebalance*: There's one member of the team who's a little aggressive and forceful, who the other more reserved team members follow. We're promoting him to Assistant Director and giving him responsibility for the team's daily deliverables, with his bonus tied to both timeliness and the quality of everyone's work. There's one position open for an additional developer. We've found a young lady with strong dev skills, some background in specific requirements, who's also social and outgoing. We've hired her to fill the position. She'll also be working with HR, leading a number of social team building events, getting the team out of the office, off the code and interacting with others. We're also adjusting bonus related milestones for each team member in support of all these efforts.

As with many of you, in personal and professional life, I've taken quite a number of personality typing, psychometry and intelligence and even some neurological tests. Myers-Briggs, PRISM, Big Five Aspects, Rorschach and the Thematic Apperception Test, Minnesota Multiphasic Personality Inventory, Rotter Incomplete Sentence Test, Wechsler Intelligence Scale for Children and the Wechsler Adult Intelligence Scale Revised, the Emotional and Social Competency Inventory, and the Mayer, Salovey, Caruso

Emotional Intelligence Test, and many others. Also, direct brain scans, such as Quantitative Electroencephalography, Single-Photon Emission Computed Tomography and digital tests for neurologic function, which come in many different forms, emphasizing different things. These to name only a few of the many tests out there in the marketplace that we may find ourselves taking in the course of our life. Some are really rather well-done, backed by solid bodies of work modeling what the inputs should be and what different outputs represent. Each gives us a little deeper insight into our intelligence and emotional quotient levels, into our personality or psychological makeup, or into how our brain is functioning at a physical level.

To be quite honest, I've never had time to dig deep enough into any of the outputs of these tests, regardless how well presented, to understand all the implications and to work out and employ how best to adapt myself to benefit fully from the knowledge attained. Actually, no one has or can. Not even test administrators and the developers. These tests only provide at best a narrow window looking out into a vastly more complex universe that is our Running Gun Battles and the war that is our life, RGBs and wars native to each of us and to our many groupings, all the way up from two people to all of humanity.

When dealing with myself, seeking proper internal control to capable of addressing current requirements, or when dealing with others. I've never once thought I should whip out Myers-Briggs results, meditate on their meaning, to then plot a thorough strategy. No one has the time for such things when running and gunning. Nor would such things provide much of an advantage even if we did have the time for detailed review and contemplation thereon. All we've time for in life, as our ever evolving RGBs play out, is to maybe pick three to five things, rapid assessment, quick plan, move out. We've no time in an actual firefight where assessment and decisions have to be made within fractions of a second. As the 5-Vectors are literally hardwired into the brain at the neurological and neuropsychological levels, as the primary Running Gun Battles evolution built right into the structures and processes of the mind. Careful thought and deliberation aren't necessary when coming to a high-fidelity assessment and plan. Merely awareness of assessment and quick course of action the brain automatically provided. Which isn't to say careful thought and deliberation aren't an important or necessary part of succeeding in RGBs and firefights. They are. Though with less thought and deliberation required of assessment and plan, far more oriented towards how to enact the plan, which is where most firefights and RGBs are lost, in the execution.

Before moving off subject of the 5-Vector Model and critical importance to success in our RGBs and firefights. We should discuss one further vector, one subtly yet very powerfully, influencing everything, this one not tied to a process. Instead being a much deeper and far older artifact riddled throughout Emotional and Cognitive Processing, influencing movement along all vectors simultaneously. This most primitive vector, hundreds of millions of years old, seemingly from the very earliest days of brains:

<u>Vector – *Compassion* ↔ *Malevolence*</u>

Introduces Unity ↔ Introduces Discordance

Given final chapter this book is specifically on Malevolence. Won't go into much detail here. Stating only a couple points. First, we can neither deny nor wish malevolence away. It too is hardwired in. Jung calling it our Shadow, going so far as to state convincingly, that we need embrace our Shadow, use it appropriately or forever be used by those who do. Second, while we may wish to believe malevolence is the root cause of RGBs and their many difficult, costly, destructive and deadly firefights, we can't. Truth is, RGBs arise from natural optimization processes built right into the brain, impossible to avoid or remove. With firefights for the most part kicking off over nothing more than a difference of opinion, a dislike, because someone skipped breakfast and is in a chemically agitated state, as well as a trillion other reasons have nothing to do with malicious intent.

Let's make no mistake, malevolence is riddled throughout all neurological processes, ancient remnant of a time before all these higher brain functions. Past where there were only two options, get along or destroy. This means even in our normal everyday run of the mill firefight, malevolence is involved, if even only subconsciously. It also means there those around us now consciously, intentionally and actively using malevolence for the power it gives them over others. Most sow discord to varying degrees, from a snide word or lie ever so carefully placed, to boldfaced lies and outright slander they rely on the weak to not challenge. A smaller percentage bring physical and psychological harm to others for the pleasure circuits it activates in the perpetrators own brain. Don't believe for a second those regularly employ malevolence are so easily identified. Virtually always, it's someone you'd never imagine using it in a lot of little ways nearly impossible to clearly define. Far more prevalent than we should care to admit, it's those sought out and attained power and authority, using this elevated and protected position to project cleverly disguised malevolence upon as many as possible. While we'd like to think malevolence is only for the incredibly small percentage of serial killers out there. It's not. This vector is resident within all of us. Only most of us have proper control mechanisms such we don't rely upon or use malevolence as the guiding vector. So, don't think for a moment you can identify those using malevolence. They've perfected their ability to hide their real intentions and actions in plain sight since they were very small children.

Rushing deeper and deeper into 21st Century Post-Industrial Era, what's required is a way in which to quick and easy, yet thoroughly, assess individuals and teams in a multivariant, multidimensional fashion, assessing mostly intangibles. The 5-Vector Model, incorporating the inescapable malevolence in interpersonal and group relationships, allows for this rapid multivariant and multidimensional assessment. This due to the Vectors being nothing more than exactly what the brain is designed to process without need for conscious thought or massive inputs. However, as is being proven now all around us, with massive disruptions and civil unrest arising from a populace trained and educated to the Industrial Era being forced to face unprepared this Postindustrial Era. What's required is more than modeling, assess and placing value on. What's required is the far harder bit, knowing how to recruit, develop and work with those incredibly few broadly skilled generalists currently exist, while seeking out and developing more of these. Something our entire system, from earliest education through to end of life, is woefully incapable of, having been purpose built over two centuries to meet the needs of industrial economies and societies. What's needed are proven models for how to select for intangibles, in order to develop and work with broadly skilled generalists.

Perfect Imperfections

"We are really competing against ourselves, we have no control over how other people perform."

— Pete Cashmore, Mashable founder and CEO

****

1584, you're born to a lesser samurai family, and raised by your father until his death when you're seven. More than four centuries later it's unclear where you received training in martial arts. However, you'll face and win first duel at age of 13. Then, age 15 you'll leave everything behind, pursuing a life of traveling and dueling. You'll go on and fight with Toyotomi Army of the West, participating in the assault on Fukushima Castle, the defense of Gifu Castle and to fight in the great Battle of Sekigahara in 1600, at age of 16. As well as in latter battles and wars.

In your life you'll fight and win 61 duels, almost twice as many as any other samurai in history, winning every single battle. After defeating the master of the greatest sword school and style in Japan, the Yoshioka, with single strike to the shoulder. You'll be challenged and will defeat the younger brother, then master. Outraged, the Yoshioka arrange a duel with final Yoshioka master, a twelve-year-old boy. To ensure revenge, Yoshioka send twelve archers, musketeers and swordsmen to ambush you. But you're not only master swordsman but also a master guerilla and truly unconventional fighter. Having arrived early and hidden yourself, you break out, and taking a sword in each hand, you kill the last Yoshioka master, and escape the ambush. Always master of the unexpected, in most of your duels you'll fight and win with nothing more than a wooden bokken and even in the single greatest battle of your life, with only a wooden oar.

Eventually, having become recognized master of the sword, of hand-to-hand combat and tactical strategy, you'll give up nomadic warrior life, life of a rōnin. Settling into service as teacher of your Nito-Ichi-ryū school of double-bladed swordsmanship developed out of immediate necessity escaping Yoshioka ambush, and as artist, philosopher and author. Master swordsman and gifted artist, it's as author you'll leave an enduring legacy, writing The Book of Five Rings, required reading of any serious warrior and strategist alike. And only weeks before your death, the Dokkōdō – Path of Aloneness – 21 precepts guided your life and pursuit of becoming a Master. Your entire life you walked a singular path, alone. Mastery of your craft being sole objective of your every moment of living. You're Musashi Miyamoto (1584-1645), living legend in your own lifetime, recognized to this day as the greatest swordsman and warrior the world has ever known. One of only a few true Masters of anything in all human history.

****

What those were educated, trained and who attained position and power in the many systems, entities, organizations and institutions of the Industrial Era find most difficult. Is that in the Postindustrial Era, it's not about getting it exactly right, precisely balancing one or more Vectors, individually or in overall team and organization. As stated, we're living in an ever more probabilistic world. This difficulty shifting from the deterministic way of thinking of the Industrial Era to far more ancient probabilistic thinking is hard enough all on its own. Given malevolence thrives in deterministic systems, on certainty, order and structure, all the many levers and tools of control manipulated for power. We're now living in a time of increased conflict as those who are driven by malevolence fight back against what they believe is a yet reversible trend to a Postindustrial world. Violence, both psychological and physical being increasingly employed as malevolence driven individuals and groupings thereof, actively pursue forcing us to return to Industrial Era models, to rigid order and structure necessary for them to retain and expand power.

Despite things will get worse before they get better. The old systems of power and its adherents ever more threatened and driven to greater degrees of violence they'll most certainly use, even if means burning the world to the ground. One only need look to the cataclysmic wars at end of the Agrarian Era as we transitioned to and through the apex of the Industrial Era last century. The transition to the Postindustrial Era is an irreversible fact. It's impossible to regulate away emergence. In highly interconnected, data and computational power rich modern world where emergence is no longer a rare, random event somewhere out there in the Human Domain. Emergent change might take decades or centuries to reach us in the old world now taking minutes or only seconds to reach millions all around our shared planet. Irrespective of the astronomical effort underway using AI and other advanced technologies to censor absolutely everything, emergence, in the name of greater security and countering 'hate speech'. This transition can't be stopped due to unpredictability and immense power of high-functioning teams emerges from the very intangibles members of these teams are selected for.

Even in the most rigid and structured environment and task in all of the last Era, it was the subtle differences, the slight incongruities of an individual or team, rather than developed regularities, provided all the advances got us to where we are now. Silicon Valley pioneers and their successful analogues, the creators of virtually all new wealth in the past thirty years, once understood this, spawning the Venture Capital industry of old. I say of old, because VC, victim of its own success, has sadly succumbed to the very same over specialization and Industrial Era thinking it once so fought and upon which its power was established. It's these intangibles, differences and incongruities, give each of us our own strengths, making possible extraordinary contributions, particularly when we combine our own with the differences and incongruities of others. Special Forces still seeks out different and irregular individuals to hone into broadly skilled generalists, relying on highly probabilistic yet sophisticated methods purpose built for this very objective. Though regrettably, SF is also quickly becoming conventional, victim of its own success and 17^+ years of general warfare that with only a handful of Global SOF units it is paying the heavy price for.

VC prior to about '07 and SF prior to about '08, understood well that in the high-Risk and Uncertainty environments they invest in, that intangibles and their combinations in a well-balanced high-functional team is the single capacity leads to success. Due the fact that unbalanced teams are incapable of predicting and leading market forces and movements. In the Postindustrial Era, the careful balancing of differences and incongruities among the members of high-functional teams alone will allow for successful address of the unknown and unexpected resulting from geometrically expanding chaos of greater complexity in the globalized economy. There's limit however to the divergence of thinking within a team that can be effective, a limit as to depth of incongruity. This because of an all-important requirement, that is, due to need for unit cohesiveness. Unit cohesiveness however, when done right, can be seeded with the original mission and purpose of the team, morphing into the emergent culture of the team itself, even better as emergent culture of a team of teams. In those rare times this happens, unique individuals brought together around a common mission and purpose, going on to become teams of these teams, most often working collaboratively as frenemies towards a shared purpose, balancing to such a high degree a successfully functioning micro-culture emerges. That's when the real magic begins!

There's an ancient Chinese saying:

– 有瑕疵鑽石價值超過沒有缺陷卵石 –

"A diamond with a flaw is worth more than a pebble without imperfections."

That's trick really, one old school VC and Green Berets alike were once masters of. Seeking out diamonds flawed in just the right way, coaching, mentoring and shaping them such the flaws unlocked tremendous value. An example. The most decorated soldier during war in Vietnam was a GB virtually no one has ever heard of, Captain Joe Hooper. Additional to the Congressional Medal of Honor, he was awarded two Silver Stars, 6 Bronze Stars with "V" Devices for actions in combat, an Air Medal, the Republic of Vietnam Gallantry Cross with Palm and eight Purple Hearts for eight separate events where he was wounded.

Joe was a troublemaker and heavy drinker with almost as many formal punishments as he had medals and awards, far more awards than those listed above, demoted several times. Despite this, he was one of the best soldiers the military has ever attracted and developed, one both saved an uncounted number of lives and who used what he knew and had learned to teach the next generation of Green Berets. Were today's SF command or civilian equivalents, HR department, to look at his personnel record in the current environment. He'd be vilified and have his hard-earned Special Forces tab revoked while being permanently forced out of the Army in disgrace.

Industrial Era minded leaders, managers and systems want perfect pebbles, not flawed diamonds. To put this in context, he would earn his MoH and later Green Beret, after already having been in trouble many times, having been booteed out of the military and fighting to get back into uniform more than once. Something inconceivable today.

Stop looking for perfect pebbles, for perfect anything, even diamonds. There aren't any. It's not there aren't diamonds without flaws. It's that these few stones have very little value in the marketplace. Which isn't a euphemism but actual real-world fact, with the diamonds of greatest market value being those with unique flaws a diamond worker meticulously highlights. Other side of this admonishment is stop seeking to be a perfect pebble, even a perfect diamond. First because it's impossible and second because it's your flaws carefully adapted and polished, are the trapped value within you. Not I'm recommending this, but I'll provide two extreme examples of flawed individuals I've known over the years who were quite literally the very best in the world at what they did. First was a cardiac surgeon, a coke fiend and unmitigated womanizer married six times, ranked as number one heart surgeon in the world for years. Second was once one of my corporate attorneys, best damn securities lawyer I've to this day ever met. And I've known more than one topline securities attorney in my line of work. He's a damn functional heroin addict. Has been for more than forty years. When there's a securities related problem no one else can fix, he can, generally after three or four days where you won't hear a thing from him. Then, out of nowhere, three AM, he'll call, give you the solution in clear, precise detail, followed the next day with appropriate legal language and related documents.

Both these men are incredibly flawed, but it's their flaws which balance their 5-Vectors and malevolence in just that right way internally, allows them to be very best in the world at what they do. They're both remarkably well-cut diamonds. However, get them outside their domain expertise and the variants thereof, and those flaws aren't of much value. In fact, these flaws become substantial hindrance and burden. While undeniably yet a diamond, outside their domain, where their internal balance and balance they bring to individuals and groups they work with, evaporates, sometimes explosively. It's not enough to be an imperfect diamond, not even flawed but perfectly cut and polished, if the individual or team isn't also thereby, perfect balance for the team or the team for your organization. Too many times I've watched as investors and SF leadership, invested in a perfect or perfectly flawed diamond only to sit by and watch as that individual or team failed. Why? Because success in the domain they were best developed to, doesn't equate to success in all or even highly related domains.

This makes the most critical task for any high-Risk and high-Uncertainty venture, that of finding or being that diamond with exact right imperfections and incongruities, honed and perfected in just the right way for the specific mission and purpose. Even if this means that finished diamond doesn't yet exist in cut and polished form and must be selected and created from raw diamond stock. Being a diamond, even cut and polished with immense success in a domain or tasking, isn't enough. As to perfect pebbles, only thing they're good for, managing what imperfect diamonds created or skipping across the mountain lake on a clear morning. Those flawless diamonds and those with too many flaws. First doesn't exist, the second, well, they get ground up and become good but expendable industrial abrasives.

Special Forces Assessment and Selection, multiweek series of mind, body and soul devouring individual and team events. Is the meticulously designed, developed and quite frequently modified, diamond in the rough selection process of SF. Of the less than 2% of the military has the temerity to try, 70% of these will fail to pass SFAS and get selected for the 18 to 26-month Special Forces Qualification Course after. With an average sticker of right around $1.5 Million getting a single individual trained sufficiently they can go on and become a Green Beret, never mind staggering costs related to all the many schools and training events required over the course of a GBs career. It's no wonder the selection process is so carefully designed, why high failure rates are not shunned, but applauded and sought. 30% failure rates in SFAS go on to 80% success rates in the SFQC. This as opposed to higher SFAS pass rates which lead to much higher failure rates in subsequent SFQC. Example, a 50% success rate in SFAS leads to 50% failure rate in SFQC. What those outside SF might find surprising is that for every selection class there are more than a few who complete everything, but after it's all over, are not selected. Reason for these "non-selects", is almost entirely due to the lack of cultural fit, despite they've proven required physical and mental capacity by completing what the vast majority of humanity won't even think about attempting. The selection process doesn't actually stop with SFAS but continues throughout a GBs career. To such a degree the most used phrase in SF is, "You're always being assessed."

Last two decades we've witnessed a still expanding number of startup selection events and programs springing up all over the world, Speed, Bunker Labs, Y Combinator and 500 Startups to name only a few. Across the board success rates are abysmal, with less than 3% of all startups entering these programs, to include those won events such as Speed and others, going on to receive necessary funding. Of those who do obtain funding, 70% fail. The first issue, low investment rates after incubator or accelerator program, or after having won in one or more startup competitions. Is due to fact only those with connections should get funded. If you don't have the connections necessary to obtain contracts for the product or service you're delivering to market, I shouldn't invest. The high failure rate issue is in large part result of investors not taking the time to really get to know the startup team, to remain involved in the startup, as active board member or advisor. Playing the numbers game instead, counting on at least one portfolio investment to hit it out of the park.

Reason most startups fail however, those few do raise funds, and reason for many others to not raise funds. Is lack of a clear culture and cultural fit. Reason for this is that it's the culture of a team, organization an institution alone, allows for 5-Vector balancing. Individuals and teams of individuals can't balance around a product or product offering, around a line of business or effort. Those few do tend to be unstable and inflexible, rather not good at being team players. Took me several failures, as founder, co-founder and investor to see the critical importance of culture. To realize it's only the culture of the team and organization made up of teams of teams the individual and individuals can balance themselves to. That is, culture being the central balance most makes sense for the team and the greater organization composed of teams, to accomplish its mission. Culture providing that floating-point around a central balance, that team members can balance themselves to.

Without a clear culture, carefully identified, developed and articulated, it's impossible to know which incongruities and imperfections are required for success. It's nearly impossible to attract the right individuals flawed and polished in all the right ways, impossible to even know what you need to look for when staffing. That is, in order to balance the team such, it's imperfect and incongruous, yet high-functional in just that way it adapts to anything, driving forward to mission success. Required hard skills are easy to identify and match.

Not so culture. Particularly if founding team hasn't thought out their culture with careful deliberation. Not only culture at founding, but as it must adapt as the startup goes through phases of growth. Virtually all my failures, and there have been far more than one, came down to this, bad cultural fit. The all-important role of culture is why SFAS emphasizes cultural fit over hard skills. It's why SF, all voluntary force, attracts the type of individuals it attracts. One thing should be noted here, from the world of Special Forces, that applies directly in startups or should. SFAS doesn't select for perfect diamonds or pebbles or even for cut, refined and polished imperfect diamonds. SFAS selects for individuals who're more than capable, a good cultural fit, even if they're yet unrefined and unfinished. Counting on SFQC and first three years on their ODA after, to complete refinement, finishing and polishing.

Without formal selection processes or the time, funding and personnel available to create just such. The need for startup team founders and co-founders specifically, to step back and think out their culture, seeded from unique 5-Vector Balance of founding team itself, becomes of paramount importance. While applicable to all, I write this with respect and yet no small measure of chagrin and chiding directly to my fellow engineers who bravely go out into the human domain and found startups. This isn't a differential calculus problem, nor a statistical regression analysis. Culture and cultural fit are a human domain problem, which makes modeling more akin to that for mapping Brownian Motion in a highly diffuse yet active gas. Seek expert help!

To help guide you in knowing which sort of help is required and what is needed of them. Or should you wish to ignore the admonishing above to seek help. There are a few specific recommendations for startups I've picked up during my time with Special Forces. Directly from the incredible cultural fit selection process SF is forever researching and improving, seeking ever more refined ways in which to map the many intangibles of a specific individual, incongruities and flaws, imperfections. More, in order to ascertain two primary things, if the individual can take instruction, can be cut, refined and polished into a diamond of great value and if the SF culture is a fit for the individual and the individual a fit for SF. The following are concepts as to team selection I certainly wish I had previous to my own startup ventures:

1- *Define your 5-Vector Balance and resultant culture*: Is your team reserved or outgoing, laid back or by the book, make it happen or follow the plan, work to play or work to work, who knows leads or who has authority leads. Knowing the balance of these will tell you what your culture is. But beware, your organic 5-Vector Balance may not be best for your team, company, market or industry. All of which matter. I'll tell you a little secret about SF, while we have a very strong culture. This culture is forever updating, driven only to a degree by internal forces, more by the types of partners, allies and customers SF serves, the missions we are tasked with, which are many, varied, and changing over time, often suddenly and dramatically;

2- *Define needs from 5-Vector Balance modeled culture*: Hard skills are easy to assess, the candidate either has them or not. Your team needs them or not. Selecting for these alone however won't tell you whether this individual is a good fit. Particularly if you need to rebalance your team such it becomes functionally better or a more general fit for your organization, market, industry, and the greater ecosystem you belong to. Work out which directions need to be moved along each Vector, develop a needs list from this further refines what a candidate must have. Word of caution, culture changes as your team changes, even without adding anyone new. What's needed of your team changes, driven by forces internal to your organization, to your network of allies and partners, to external market forces, regulatory changes, and a vast web of directly and indirectly impactful influences. This necessitates reassessment of your team's culture prior to each time you make personnel or direction changes;

3- *Develop individualized scenario-based assessments*: Okay, so now you know what your culture is, your 5-Vector Balance, how it needs adapting and what you're looking for in a candidate. Great, on to the hardest part, seeking out, attracting, connecting with and assessing the individual or individuals. It's impossible to know who someone is and will be looking at static data from yesterday or even a pattern in data going back to the beginning of one's life and career. Nor from responses to questionnaires and clever brain games. Only way to know who someone is, their 5-Vector Balance, is if you confront them with an appropriate challenge while putting them under stress. The many RGBs of startups, and the inevitable series of firefights will ensue in the daily life of each of your teammates necessitate you properly assess candidates carefully. There's no better way to do this than to give them a scenario to find solutions for, related specifically to what they would be doing on your team. Even better if it is a Kobayashi Maru style scenario, broken into segments, each of which requires its own solutions before one can progress. You're hiring these people to solve problems for you. Give them one of your worst in the hiring process. See how they do;

4- *Involve more than only final decision makers*: It's always the case, most everyone on the team is far too busy to stop and participate in the selection process. But guess what, there's no other way to ensure proper team fit, unless the team, at least enough senior members of, are involved in the selection process, directly. Given the operational tempo for Special Forces, any given day in an average of 95 nations, sometimes as many as 125, it would be far more effective to outsource the entire selection process to a contracted entity which did only that. But we don't and can't. Reason is, only those drawn from ODAs and going back to ODAs to serve alongside those being selected. Cadre who've served in a sufficient number of roles, deployed in a sufficient number of locales, conducted a sufficient number of operations and operational types to truly understand life on and ODA and in SF. Only these can understand the culture and know what's needed to sustain and evolve that culture. More critically, only they know what to look for given today's SF culture and how it needs adapt in the term of their career. Even more critically though, and why it can't be only one or two team members and ultimate decision-maker or only the decision-maker. Is that no one individual is capable of fully assessing a human being. None of us can see everything, this even less all the time, and we've each our own cognitive biases to deal with which at times do mean we unfairly judge. Only a team of candidate selectors, a team derived of those from the very team being selected for, is capable of the task. Each looking at key aspects during the scenario challenge, each assessing in their own fashion and for their own Vectors. Best choice is to involve different team members in different parts of the scenario-based assessment, those parts they have most direct experience with and in the conduct of, will have to work with the hired individual doing.

5-   *Use data generated but trust instincts*: Take notes, make running assessments, confer with teammates, adapt your assessment as the event goes along. Document all of it thoroughly. Compile into a matrix everyone's assessments, key comments and decisions made throughout the event and at pivotal points. Derive a hard analysis from the data as to the suitability of the candidate. If they are a go on all the hard data points. Or enough of. Set them aside completely and trust the instincts of each team member. There is a powerful reason why SFAS team week events are broken into segment pieces, with a different Cadre member assessing during each different segment. While hard data points can be tabulated and valued, even if argued over, it's invariably the case, that intangibles far outweigh any and all of these data points, no matter how cleverly devised. It's true, an individual may, right or wrong, assess another individual in a single event or at a single place in time, leading to incorrect skewing. Hell, you could've just rubbed wrong at the wrong time, such, without any conscious thought, you're biased against by an individual at all times thereafter. Trust the instincts of your team members to pick up on all those intangibles, the perfect imperfections necessary for the successful conduct of the RGBs your team is involved in. Just do so balancing across several team members and not only any single team member.

Just know, even SF, with its comprehensive SFAS selection process, makes mistakes, selects candidates to continue on to the Qualification Course who're not right match, for either themselves or the Regiment. This due to fact there's simply no such thing as perfect knowledge a priori. And to the fact we naturally bias towards wanting to work with our fellow humans, particularly those we respect for their backgrounds and capacities, or only because we've taken a liking to them. In this case, where the selection process came up short, and an individual joins the team who isn't a good fit, it's best to sever the relationship at the soonest opportunity and this as amicably as possible so that both the team and the individual may go on and prosper. Don't need to inadvertently create and take on yet another RGB.

Selecting for Intangibles

"Don't be cocky. Don't be flashy. There's always someone better than you."

— Tony Hsieh, Zappos CEO

****

You're born to a mother of Yadav Royal family and to father who is both Maratha general and guerilla warfare supporter, serving Deccan Sultanates. In your early years you'll grow up under Islamic Mughal rule, your father, Shahaji Bhonsel, being trusted general and administrator of the Bijapur Sultanate. Despite this, in 1645 at the age of 16, you'll express in a letter the concept of Hindavi Swaraiya –

Indian Self-Rule. Same year, through bribery or coercion, you assume command of Torna Fort. With Torna Fort as your base you will then begin raids against Bijapuri forces and strongholds, taking lands and fortifications, building up an army before seizing the Valley of Javali.

1657, your attentions shift to the Mughals despite previous good relations. Employing guerilla tactics, you'll survive battles against far superior numbers, even defeating an enemy stronghold with 200 men, disguised as wedding guests. This before finally being defeated and forced to become a Mughul vassal giving up much of your forts and forces. 1670, you turn again against the Mughals, who are busy fighting the Afghans, retaking much of the lands and forts you'd surrendered. 1674, after tenuously being declared descendent of Kshatriya family, you'll be crowned the Hindu sovereign of the Hindu Marathas, under the Vedic rights. This in a land and time dominated and ruled by Muslim Mughals.

After being crowned, you'll turn your attentions to Southern India, to bringing all peoples of the Deccan under a single rule, a Hindu rule. Your Marathan armies, in alliance with fellow Deccan rulers, will conquer much of Southern India, to include the lands held by your half-brother. From this you'll establish a dynasty will war with the Mughals until eventual Mughal defeat in 1707. A dynasty which birthed the Marathi Confederacy will reign until defeat at hands of British East Indies Company in 1805.

You'll reintroduce Marathi and Sanskrit languages, replacing the Persian of the Mughals. You'll reintroduce Hindu courtly and political traditions, support scholars and Hindu scholarship. And will introduce a highly effective administrative system by which to govern the large territories and populations under your command. You're Shivaji Bhonsle (1627-1680), and you'll break your people free of Muslim rulers and will inspire, two centuries later, the Indian peoples under British rule, to seek their identity, and to once more become an independent people.

****

Intangibles, intangibles! Everyone's all about the intangibles. Talk to any HR department, recruiter or headhunter, virtually any expert in the field, they'll tell you how good they are at identifying and selecting for intangibles. Look more closely and 99.999% of the time what you'll see being measured are tangibles all mashed together with a patchwork of feel good subjective nonsense. Most of which is nothing more than a clever justification for why the individual responsible for hiring didn't take the candidate actually best suited for the particular job. This because the one doing the hiring can't overcome their own cognitive biases and so creates elaborate models supposedly allow for measuring intangibles. When in fact the model does nothing but protect hiring personnel who turn down those they just don't like. Here's a little fact, you can't measure intangibles. Not directly. Intangibles are much like dark energy and matter, invisible to the eye, but recognized in the gravitational warping of what can be seen. In their influence on mission success, which always means, in their influence within the team and across teams. Couple examples are in order.

Employed a software developer to be our quality assurance coder, many years ago. His resume was impeccable. Though, in a private conversation with a friend of mine he'd worked for, friend told me to watch out. This developer did great work but rarely showed up, causing more disruption in the dev team than he was worth. Overlooking this, we brought him in for an interview. He did incredibly well. Everyone liked him and wanted to work with him. After about three months, he just stopped showing up regularly. This before telecommuting was a thing. Days he did show, he'd put on his headphones, talk to no one, only staying a few hours. Most of our dev team were becoming more and more pissed, and the whole thing was beginning to cause a stir among the entire startup team. I put an end to all that. Why? Because when it came to fixing code, he was a Rockstar.

One night over drinks, where I was seriously entertaining letting him go, he told me bluntly his best thinking happened when he was surfing. When he didn't show in the office, he was out on the waves figuring out some complex problem, only to come in and within a few hours fix it. Quite often rewriting hundreds of lines of code sprinkled throughout the codebase. Fixing problems entire dev team couldn't, often knowing the problem merely from detailed understanding of each team member, the way they approached code writing, where their code was in the larger codebase and how it interacted with the code of others and the whole. It was an intricate game for him. He loved and thrived on the challenge of solving what others couldn't, and in no small measure on the disruption caused by his Rockstar status, higher pay, direct access to and influence with startup founder, only showing up when he wanted to, in hours fixing what others spent days and weeks trying to figure out.

After months working on architecture of their B2B platform, staffing up dev, marketing and sales teams, preparing to go to market. Startup team leadership of one of our investments, kept running up against problems with vendors and partners required of their platform. They'd tried everything but were small players in a big marketplace. These major vendors and partners didn't need to care about adjusting deliverables and pricing just for this startup, irrespective how credible and connected the startup investors were. The founders stopped being able to reach any of the decision-makers at these firms. Which if it continued, would lead to certain failure. There was one person we knew with all the right connections in all but one of the vendors and partners required. But she was difficult at best. Someone I personally didn't like at all. But she was damned good and I respected her for that. We made an introduction to the startup founders, carefully protecting ourselves, saying only she possessed the right relationships. Though the founders would have to determine all on their own if she was a good fit.

True to form she so angered the founder I received a call immediately after their first meet at a coffee shop in Palo Alto. She'd bluntly told him they were nobody and there was no reason why these major Silicon Valley firms should even meet with him, as it would be a waste of time. She called me less than an hour later, telling me what she thought of the founder. Wasn't flattering. Thought he was a naïve fool, yet another engineer thought his superior innovation would far more than compensate for his lack of social acumen. Hell, his solution was the best there was in the world and everyone would fall all over themselves for it. Which as with so many other startups, including my first, proved not to be the case.

Turns out she'd been hired by a competitor to our investment for much the same reason. She'd rubbed that founder wrong as well and been let go a week before the vesting cliff for her options. Oh, and one of the reps for a vendor our startup had failed to gain attention of, had also angered her a year prior. She wanted to see startup had let her go, fail, and competitor to the rep had insulted her, get a major contract and lose out on a very large opportunity. There was no way she was going to work for another founder she didn't have much respect for, knowing she'd get fired once problem was solved, but she'd accept very well-compensated consulting agreement. Out of desperation the founder agreed and over the four months she got them exactly what they needed, even better than they had planned or projected. All the while angering a whole lot more people absolutely everywhere she went. Measurable tangibles certainly weren't what motivated her to incredible professional successes, and she had many spread across her career. Simple fact is that quite unlike most of us, she was unabashedly motivated by anger and hate her entire life, thriving on the chaos she created, intentionally.

There's no possibility of me detailing for you the intangibles made both individuals so successful in these two instances. I can say with complete confidence the intangibles for each emerged from their own internal 5-Vector Balancing and the rebalancing this provided teams they worked with. SFAS, in seeking a whole of person approach to selection, models six primary attributes: intelligence; trainability; physical fitness; motivation; influence; and judgement. Not a bad list to start with for startups, even the physical fitness attribute. While these are all things which can be objectively measured, what makes them intangibles is the manner in which measurement is derived. Not from a one size fits all, though minimums are standardized. Rather, SFAS assesses the individual based on themselves, assigning values may well place the individual higher than peers, despite these same peers having received a higher score in that event. It's individual assessment of seasoned and experienced cadre members, averaged across all events and assessments made by different cadre over time. That allows for both tangible and intangible measure.

When it comes to startup leaders and teams, additional to the SFAS list, I also look for the following:

-       Overabundant ambition – *We only rise to the level of our ambition* – If we aren't hungry for extraordinary success, particularly when set against very high likelihood of failure, we will not dig deep enough into ourselves to put in the long, hard, often thankless hours, months and years, necessary to realize our ambition;

-       Extreme sociability – *We're only as strong as our network* – No ODA, startup team, organization, government or corporation is a self-contained, self-supported totalitarian dictatorship isolated on a remote and protected island, which requires us to quickly establish and adapt relationships with nearly anyone, no matter personality differences or historical animosities;

-       Inability to quit – *We accomplish only what we believe we can* – Unwavering Tenacity, perhaps the single most important of all intangibles, must exist as everyone is eager and ambitious when things are progressing well but often catastrophically not so when things are going badly, as they will in high-Risk and Uncertainty environments;

-       Myopic focus – *We only attain what we see clearly through the noise* – Even with all three of the above, success requires we stay on a singular path, often moving to a point only we see, quantum walks don't make sense to anyone else requiring unwavering attention to the final destination, focus allows both for dogged determination as well as an ability to foresee threats in time to respond; And most critically,

- Driven by failure – *We only evolve through substantial personal failure* – Unless we can accept failure or the threat of failure as a lesson learned leading to ultimate success in the future, we simply don't possess the frame of mind necessary to continue when everyone and everything, including our demons, are telling us it can't be done.

It's only been in the last two years, after a decade in SF, four years doing Computational Engineering studies, developing the 5-Vector Model. That I've come to fully appreciate the value of intangibles, of those things I simply can't measure in any linear or direct fashion. The Hidden Markov Chains of human engagement, if you will. Where before, a couple decades, I spent considerable time analyzing the concept, the market, the team and financial pro forma. Data, data, data, followed by modeling, modeling, modeling. I now spend majority my time with a startup team, getting to know their 5-Vector Balance, their imperfections, individually and as a team. Doing this by walking through difficult scenarios I've developed directly from those things they'll directly face in pursuit of their particular startup, in its particular ecosystem and market. Asking hard questions, politely and sometimes in a confrontational manner, gauging responses, assessing for those many imperfections, intangibles I can't really see other than in the individual and team 5-Vector Balance.

Increasingly, I seek to ensure startup founders or leadership has the understanding and skills to do this very probing and assessing themselves. Emphasizing necessity to truly know the market they're creating or entering, know the players and competitors, what they're doing, how they'll respond to this new entrant, what externalities influence behavior internal to that industrial segment and across all the segments it touches upon. In fact, I now assess almost solely for startup leaders who recognize business is total, unrelenting warfare. Who, accept this and continually plan and self-adjust themselves accordingly, frequently. Who recognize success in total war comes from a relentless series of nonlinear, nondeterministic, often random appearing quantum walks around observing, intuiting and recognizing intangibles, integrated with quick modeling and planning, followed immediately with rapidly adjusting team and leadership internal and external balances. I need teams who know that to prevail in firefights and to successfully sustain the RGBs these fights are embedded within. Requires staying ahead of the competition, market forces and the inevitable tendency to self-deception arises from complacency and over confidence.

Intangibles, intangibles, intangibles! As the old saying goes, "Can't create the required intangibles in those don't possess them already. But if the intangibles do exist in an individual. That individual can be mentored to success in most anything." This is true with the individual and with teams. Startup teams specifically. In fact, while absolutely essential each member of the team in a very early-stage startup possesses their own additive intangibles in order they may contribute maximally to the success of their startup. It's even more important the team as a whole possesses its own combinative intangibles and emergent 5-Vector balance. Over the decades I've seen more startups fail because they didn't understand they were only a small part of a much larger ecosystem of investors, vendors, partners, allies, customers, regulatory bodies, and the list goes on nearly ad infinitum. I've seen great teams with great products and services, fail to penetrate the market, or even to get to market. Because of this one thing. The 5-Vector Balance of their team, its intangibles and the resultant culture, wasn't a good fit for their ecosystem.

One Among Many

"The most dangerous poison is the feeling of achievement. The antidote is to every evening think what can be done better tomorrow."

— Ingvar Kamprad, IKEA founder

* *

Early on you demonstrate the bravery will follow you all your life. This age 12, taming, Bucephalus the enormous, wild stallion with a furious demeanor. Aristotle is your teacher, sparking a lifelong fascination with literature, science, medicine and philosophy. At age of 16, while your father is away, you'll lead your cavalry in defeat of the Sacred Band of Thebes, previously believed to be undefeatable. Already a proven strategist, by age 20 you're king, killing any and all rivals before they challenge your claim to the throne, while quelling rebellions among conquered peoples.

By age 23 you've conquered the great Persian armies in the Battle of Issus. Additional to bravery, you demonstrate a shrewd tactical mind, employing innovative tactics and strategies and guerilla warfare to defeat far superior forces time and time again. You'll finally conquer the Persian empire, before entering Punjab, India. Then, after defeating King Porus at Hydaspes River, your forces, exhausted after years of conquest and battle, will rebel. Leading you to split your forces, dedicated portions to rule regions of your empire. Your reign of conquests birthing dynasties across much of the then known world.

You're Alexander the Great (356-332BCE), charismatic-ruthless, power hungry-diplomatic, brilliant and bloodthirsty, driven to unite all the peoples of the world. Undefeated strategist, you're a leader, inspiring utter loyalty. Recognized to this day as one of the most influential individuals to have ever lived. By time of your death at age of 32, you'll rule largest empire the ancient world had yet seen, stretching from Greece to Northwestern India. Your legacy of cultural diffusion and syncretism spawned an era, the Hellenistic Era and such powerful belief systems as Greco-Buddhism. You'll found 20 cities bore your name, and the Great Library of Alexandria, this while spreading Greek influence will be evident as late as 15th Century in Byzantium traditions and in Greek speakers in Central and Eastern Anatolia into the 1920s. You'll become the metric against which all future generals are assessed, with your innovative tactics and strategies taught in military academies around the world to this day.

****

New GBs "Cool Guys" and first-time startup founders "Cool Kids" suffer from very same malady. Both believing they're the absolute center of the known universe, critical tip of the spear. Neither recognizing they're little more than bit players contributing an infinitesimally small piece to a much larger effort. In the world of SpecOps, any given mission is nothing more than one part of an ever-evolving global strategy, no matter how critical or pivotal the mission may be. While in the world of startups, your product or service is a small part of the larger industrial segment you're in, which itself is only a part of the larger still industry and this too is only a small part of the overall ecosystem your industrial segment and industry belong to. All of these have their own personality, culture, their own 5-Vector balance, a composite of all the players directly and indirectly engaged with one another in the increasingly globalized supply chain and marketplace. All of which changes over time, ever more suddenly and dramatically, as the rest of the world steadily "comes online", so's to speak.

Twenty years ago, my co-founder and I believed we were going to change everything. We had the very best product and solution in the world at the time and as revolutionaries, we were going to use our innovation to substantially improve quality and lower costs for data centers, telecommunications meet me rooms, peering points and the lot of it. While we were right about our advances being the best there was for the time, my co-founder Brad's network design a third the cost and twice as resilient and capable. This all vetted by major telecom vendors and partners during our build up and go to market efforts. We had a private investment group as backers, active investors, fully in support of our efforts, as well as major partners, vendors and access to leading Tier One clients. We had the perfect solution for all. Or so we thought. Ultimately, we failed. Why you might ask?

Market participants neither need nor want perfect solutions. Perhaps the hardest lesson I've learned, requiring failure of my second startup in telecom. Turns out perfect solutions, lowest prices, and all the plentitude of reasons entrepreneurs believe make their product irresistible. Turn out to not be the factors ultimately drive participant decisions. Major clients, partners and vendors alike most often don't care about costs or quality improvements. Leastwise not enough to switch from their current providers or solutions. What they care about are intangibles, your 5-Vector Balance, if this makes you that most elusive of things, a "good market fit". This last having far less to do with your product or service than you would imagine. Having far more to do with your team, your startup as a whole and whether its culture is a good fit for the ecosystem. This even more so if your offering is disruptive.

Putting it bluntly, you must fit naturally into the RGBs of the ecosystem, capable of prevailing in the many firefights will occur as these RGBs play out over time.

Having once played at being a "Cool Guy." I've helped develop and have sat through endless mission briefs laying out in detail, perfect plans with perfect strategies to perfectly effect truly intractable problems. Perfect solutions could and would individually turn the tide of war. A lot of these plans actually were just that, perfect or as close to as is humanly possible. At least with respect to specific targets. Green Berets as ODAs are the world's undisputed foremost experts on intelligence gathering, analysis, course of action dev and wargaming, followed by near flawless execution. Most plans were never approved, greatly angering the team pitching. A team rarely understanding reasons for the denial, believing their solution to be only plan capable of getting the win and changing the course of the war, even that war fought in the shadows.

Prior to time in SF, as entrepreneur and investor, I'd seen the same many times. With most attempts to attain funding, never getting to full pitch, if getting to pitch at all. The vast majority never making it that far. Just as with the Cool Guys, the Cool Kids, my team and I in my early career and most all startup teams have pitched me since. Wrongly believe if only the investor understood how revolutionary their offering is, how much the market will love and adopt it. Problem is, we very often do, knowing well disruption will be caused in the ecosystem we invest in. That's if the innovative offering is ever adopted at all, most never realizing customer adoption, particularly not the disruptive ones. That is, unless the team startup and ODA alike, recognizes and has planned for the disruptions will be caused in successful execution of their plan. This disruption planning taking into account all those directly involved and several levels out in all directions.

That is, taking into account all the RGBs and many firefights everyone in your marketplace and its greater ecosystem, are engaged in, how your offering changes the nature of these. Taking into account different personalities of the entities and decision-makers, composed of the intangibles compose the 5-Vector Balances of individuals, teams and organizations. As we say in SF, know Commander's Intent two levels up and always plan for intended and unintended second and third order effects. Known knowns, known unknowns and unknown unknowns all taken into account, emphasis on people rather than your particular offering. What most all teams, startups and ODAs alike fail to understand is if they don't do all this. Many layered multidimensional analyses, planning, wargaming and strategy development, command or investor, anyone of any import in the ecosystem really, can't join, approve or back your effort.

Despite Cool Guys and Cool Kids are driven by cockiness derived from lack of experience, heavy specialization or just by nature of those drawn to such lines of work. Individuals and teams believing they're the center of the Universe, that their solution alone will change it all. A cockiness needs be allowed to some degree or they won't have the balls to do what they must, take on incredible Risks and Uncertainties. Never-the-less, despite all this, both have something to offer one another and more established and larger organizations.

- Erroneous in belief their mission will change course of the war, Cool Guys, yet do understand need for allies, supporting efforts, detailed planning, collaboration, all to win hearts and minds of the people, gaining and holding the Human Domain, through sophisticated messaging, resource and credit sharing and surgically precise violence. This while always prepared to move immediately to follow-on missions, making course corrections where necessary, as required by environmental conditions. Understanding they operate in someone else's battlespace, that victory isn't theirs but instead belongs to the far bigger mission playing out with forces vastly larger than just their 12-man team, often forces and efforts wrapping around the entire planet and involved hundreds of thousands of participants in hundreds and even thousands of entities each with their own required outcomes.

- Though virtually always overvaluing importance of their offering, Cool Kids are yet masters of creating assets from little more than ideas and concepts, assets realize real, measurable returns for both stakeholders and shareholders. Creating assets out in incredibly hostile environments with little to no support, introducing order out of chaos, if with a disruptive solution, forcing new organizational structuring into an industrial segment and ecosystem doesn't want to change. This while having to develop from virtually nothing, the culture, 5-Vector Balance of intangibles, required that they become a contributing participant in the many RGBs of the market they belong to, capable of holding their own in any firefight.

Tomorrow's economic system and its many participants are neither capable of nor are they seeking perfect solutions. They're seeking best solutions possible given all the many involved, decision-makers, consumers, regulators, the lot of it. This at every level. Decisions upon decisions, which have to be made, with price and quality being only two of many considerations, neither even the most critical considerations. This means the course of industries, business ecosystems, and wars alike, never change by the introduction of a perfect product or battle but by the interplay of all those many decisions settled upon. Decisions never made in a vacuum but in context of highly fluid and complex, often competing, business and even more importantly social obligations where there's no main effort, no definitive end or win.

It's not enough to get balance right in your team, that balance of intangibles make your team highly capable and productive. You can have the best functioning and most deadly team out there in the marketplace, winning every single firefight they get into, and still lose. Lose because it's not about you and your team, ODA or startup. That's point right there! The one most of us miss as we carefully learn and develop ourselves into the best self we can, individually and as teams. Point is, there's no main effort, no decisive action. Only a very large collaborative effort we're nested within, as one of the many contributing members thereof, effort continues indefinitely. There's only time sensitive, context relevant decisions have to be made, decisions marginally related to price or quality, to business at all. This reality requires we get over ourselves and start looking at our teams and offerings in context of all the many individuals and entities have to make decisions in order for our offering to become a contributing part of much larger and now global market. In particular, we have to put in the time and energy to understand and deliberately prepare our teams for the environmental and social context in which investors, shareholders and stakeholders, vendors, partners, clients and their clients make decisions, all of which extend far beyond business alone.

Team Types

"If you can't feed a team with two pizzas, it's too large."

— Jeff Bezos, Amazon founder and CEO

****

Descendant of Maille mac Conall, you're born into Irish Nobility, Claire Island in Clew Bay, County Mayo, 1530. Your father is Lord of the Ó Máille dynasty and ruler of Umall. As a young girl, to shame your father into taking you on sailing expedition to Spain, you'll cut your long hair to not allow it to get caught in ropes. Demonstrating a pattern of defiance will remain throughout your life. Upon your father's death, rather than your brother Dónal an Phíopa Ó Mháille, you'll assume active leadership of the Lordship, ruling by land and sea.

1546, you'll marry **Dónal an Chogaidh Ó Flaithbheartaigh**, heir to the Ó Flaithbheartaigh title. Your eldest son Eoghan will be tricked and murdered by Sir Richard Bingham, Queen Elizabeth's appointed Lord President of Connacht. Your daughter Méadhbh, cut from the same cloth, will come to your rescue more than once, saving your life. Upon the death of **Dónal, you'll return to Clare Island**, to Granuaile's Castle. Picking up the nickname "Dark Lady of Doona" after assaulting Doona Castle, killing your lover's murderers. You'll marry a second time, to **Risdeárd an Iarainn Bourke**, 1st Viscount Mayo being the son born of this marriage.

You're Gráinne Ní Mháille "Grace O'Malley" (1530-1603). For forty years you'll defy English and Irish claims to your lands, to lordship over your people. Master of guerrilla warfare on land and at sea, you'll fight an unconventional war your entire life. Sir Richard Bingham would state in response to your petition against him to Her Majesty Queen Elizabeth I, you were *"nurse to all rebellions in the province for this forty years"*. Irish historian and novelist, Anne Chambers describes you as, *"a fearless leader, by land and by sea, a political pragmatist and politician, a ruthless plunderer, a mercenary, a rebel, a shrewd and able negotiator, the protective matriarch of her family and tribe, a genuine inheritor of the Mother Goddess and Warrior Queen attributes of her remote ancestors. Above all else, she emerges as a woman who broke the mould and thereby played a unique role in history."*

****

That the team's everything in a startup, or any organization operating in high-Risk and high-Uncertainty environments, has been stated to such degree now it's getting close to cliché. Before losing all value as guidance, let's shift gears. I've not discussed the types of individuals you require on your team, the type of individual you should model yourself after. That will all come in the third book on person development. If you simply can't wait and need to get a grasp on the topic of individuals, take a look at Stephanie Vozza's solid piece in *Fast Company*, The Only Six People You Need on Your Founding Startup Team.

Instead of banging on about the importance of a great startup team, let's talk about the different team types and how the appropriate team might be assembled using guidance from the startup team of Special Forces, the ODA. There are a great number of team types out there, each optimized for a given domain, such as: sports, technology and product development, academic research, philanthropy, corporations, government agency, social services, law enforcement and emergency services, to name only a few of the hundreds of thousands of teams, each with their very own unique culture and internal cohesion. Beth Miller in her 2012 article in *Business 2 Community* 7 Team Types That Make Business Possible, identified the types of teams most appropriate for the business environment of startups, but which apply to any teams really:

    i)   Functional Teams;
    ii)   Cross-functional Teams;
    iii)   Leadership Teams;
    iv)   Self-directed Teams;
    v)   Virtual Teams;
    vi)   Quality Circles; And
    vii)   Task Forces.

While any real success will ultimately require all seven team types, startups rarely, if ever, have the luxury of assembling the number and types of individuals necessary to compose and drive these seven teams to a singular success. ODA's, as only 12-man elements, never do, and yet still must address every team type and need. As with ODAs, in the early days your startup team will be limited though it must address all team type needs. ODAs benefit from the greater SpecOps community and can outsource some of these requirements. Startups rarely ever have even this modest luxury. Perhaps more appropriate to startups would be the book *Discipline of Teams*. This though I disagree with selecting for skills rather than compatibility, when it comes to early-stage startups. That is, where the stress levels are immense, resources and manpower limited and where you'll be living all up in one another's lives daily. As is the case with deployed ODAs. In the book, Katzenbach and Smith identified there are really only three distinct, overarching, team types:

i)   Teams that recommend things;
ii) Teams that make or do things; And
iii) Teams that run things.

Prior to attaining authorization to conduct any mission, the ODA must first devise an incredibly detailed plan of action and recommend their solution. When authority is attained, they must then make all of the many moving pieces involved in that solution come together before going on to conduct the mission. An incredibly detailed effort, a staggering volume of work completed prior to every single mission by the 12-man ODA. This as we're by design and doctrine, a fully self-contained fighting force, purpose built to operate alone and unsupported behind enemy lines for months and years if necessary. All of this prior to then going on to lead the effort, the mission. Often right in the very heart of enemy territory, carving out order, developing assets, in hostile environments. Missions which can run for hours, days, weeks, months and even years.

In practice, your startup team needs to be capable of moving between all three of these at any given moment, as dictated by current market reality, all without ability to make major team changes. This is true of an ODA as well, with much the same internal dynamics, constraints and limitations. With the battlespace and threat evolving rapidly, requiring sudden movement between all three team types. Hell, most times, having to run all three concurrently. In a high-functional startup team and ODA alike, what makes this critical flow between team types possible, is the unique combination of personalities, mastery of individual occupational skills and further specialty skills as well as individual and collective histories of practical application of both. Let's not leave out the absolute requirement for a productive 5-Vector Balance allows for shared culture that puts the mission and the team, rather the individual, first.

While quite similar in their requirements. There are of course dynamics unique to ODA's, dynamics if applied by startup founding leaders, makes them far more capable of shifting between or concurrently running all three team types. In the private sector, particularly in startups, most often composed of youthful individuals with little life experience outside school and their startup. It's nearly impossible to match the starting conditions provide ODA's with their incredibly powerful internal cohesion. Namely the shared experiences of having gone through a brutal selection process and the grueling and lengthy school thereafter. This followed by many deployments and additional skills schools, leading to extensive practical experience and a vast array of individual capabilities and shared experiences, as the individual and as member of at least one high-functional team. This, having made transition between three team types many times, often leading some of these changes and teams. Despite we can't be taking startup founding teams through SFAS and SFQC nor through an equivalent, there are some of the dynamics make GBs so capable, can be adopted.

- *Different answers needed* – Recommend, Make/Do Things and Run Things team types require their own, often very different answers, to address their own particular needs. Reach into that diverse background of skills and experiences in your overall startup team, including investors and advisors, seek out those with the right answers for the mode you're in or shifting into;

- *Different leader needed* – Due to the way the human brain wires, each of us is strong in only one of the three team types, with our brain wired for persuasion, for labour or for managing. While there must be overall leadership, employ a horizontal organizational, with the individual most wired or with the most experience for the team type, leading or at least directly involved, when your startup is in that team mode;

- *Different skills needed* – While we each are wired for contributions to a type of team, evolutionary specialization, it's still best everyone cross-trains in the skillsets required of all three. Mastery of a team type that isn't by nature ours, is a stretch. However, we must at all times still be prepared to contribute and even lead at a moment's notice, recognizing that at any point in life we may be called upon to do just that;

- *Different personalities needed* – Whether identifying which team type is most natural to you, or if you're preparing to develop yourself in another. Or if you're having to take on leadership. Know, each type requires a different personality, a different Vector balancing. Get the balance wrong, fail to match personality right for team type, and often, no matter how good individuals involved are, they'll fail;

- *Different struggles needed* – Dirty little secret about high-functional teams. There're always fights and conflicts. Guess what. These struggles are essential. It's only way for teams, regardless of their type, to make major contributions. There's one hard fast rule, however. Members must be able to implicitly trust, what happens in the team stays in the team, conflicts and problems dealt with internally and those fail to adhere to this find their $hit in the hall, are off the team; And

- *Different mindset needed* – You may be good at a team type, skilled at others. You may cause and embrace the conflicts and struggles necessary for success. But if you don't have a thick skin. You're useless and shouldn't be on any team. It's essential, on all high-functional teams, to hear things you don't want to hear about yourself. This isn't a matter of don't dish out what you can't take. F%$# that! For good of the team, each and every one of us needs to at times say and receive the really hard things, those truths absolutely critical to the team's success. This from leadership and any team member, even lowest and newest member of the team.

While it may not be possible in the startup world to replicate unique conditions that lead to a Special Forces ODA, it's still quite possible to build a solid team with many of the very same dynamics. Having been so fortunate as to have been on both successful and unsuccessful startup teams, and having spent years on both successful and not successful ODAs, I'd put forward few recommendations for team related efforts, assembling and developing your people for any and all of the three team types:

- *Answers*: Regardless team type, ensure each member of the team resonates with the Founder's vision, the startup's mission and thoroughly understands the goals of the team;

- *Leaders*: While selecting individuals for their base of experience derived skills and capabilities, make sure to also have team members and leaders available for each team type;

- *Skills*: In ever-changing world of startups, cross train your people so they can rapidly shift to and contribute or lead any type of team, even to more than one type at a time;

- *Personalities*: We can change our own balance along one or more Vector a little, making getting personality mix of the team essential for high-functional teams of any type;

- *Struggles*: Nature of struggles required of each team type are different, changing over time, so select those willing to fight if required, but who pick their fights very carefully;

- *Mindsets*: Doesn't matter for a team type or all types, recruit and develop, those seek truth about self, specifically hard truth, kind of truth hurts and forces us to make changes.

Being a contributing member of a team is always a difficult task for anyone, even the most social. Particularly when that team is tasked with a critical mission must be accomplished in a timely fashion, in a hostile environment and with highly constrained resources, which is always the case in the world of startups and ODA's. Ensuring you've assembled the right team, a team capable of moving back and forth between recommending, doing and running things, is absolutely essential to success. Building a team that wants to work together to accomplish a shared purpose is even more critical, requiring thick skinned individuals don't take disagreement or criticism personally, as their singular focus is on success in the marketplace over their own success. Trick to this last, for the individual, is to know that our personal success is first team success. Might as well focus on team and its mission above all other concerns.

Hard Learned

"A person who is quietly confident makes the best leader."

— Fred Wilson, Union Square Ventures co-founder

****

Born later years of the Han Dynasty, in Qiao County, Pei Prefecture, descendent of Xiaohou Ying. You'll early demonstrate a righteous but violent nature. At the age of 14, killing a man dishonored your teacher. Having already proven yourself, Cao Cao will appoint you as his strategic advisor, before promoting you to Zhechong Xiaowei and then governor of Dong Prefecture.

Riding to the defense of Cao Cao's family, you are betrayed and taken hostage by some of your own men. After your rescue, in which all the hostage takers were slaughtered without mercy. Setting a precedent exists to this day, even it if means death of the hostages, kill any and all who would take others hostage.

You'll lose an eye in an attack on Lü Bu, famously having plucked the arrow and eye from your skull, eating the eye and continuing with the battle. Again you'll be promoted, to governor of Chenliu and Jiyin, later of He'nan, given the title of Jianwu Jiangjun, and knighted as Duke of Gao An Xiang, title your descendants will inherit. As governor the people will thrive, even during draughts where you and your men will damn and divert rivers, working with your own hands like a peasant. Such is esteem among lord and peasant alike, your contributions will be officially recorded. You'll be awarded 4,300 households under your command, 26 army units and many famous musicians and dancers. Upon Wei Wen Di inheriting the title of Prince of Wei, you'll be promoted to Great General, months before your death.

You're Xiahou Dun (?-220AD) and while not one to shy from violence, proving yourself as a great military thinker and leader, you'll be remembered most for your humility and life spent as a student, as a wise advisor. An exceedingly wealthy man, you and your descendants will forever be remembered as staunch defender and champion of the people, giving of your own wealth to the masses, in times of shortage taking from the treasury to help the peasants. Given the title of Loyal Duke upon your death, you're the very epitome of Nobility.

****

Though I played a year of football in high school, for most part participated in solitary sports, distance running, skiing and later triathlons. This due to reclusive nature and that I've believed since earliest years, only real competition is with ourselves of yesterday. Combination of both meant later in life I'd approach all endeavours, whether business, personal or athletic, as individual sports to be accomplished through substantial personal dedication and effort almost solely. This mindset carried with me through my first two Silicon Valley startups and later as an analyst and investment advisor. In the good times it worked quite well. However, when things got hard, as always do, this individual effort mindset became an insurmountable hindrance to success. If only I'd known life was such a team sport when young. Might have made a few different choices. Might is optimal word, as I never planned on being in business or finance.

Regardless, after nearly twenty years in business and finance, this same mindset went with me into Special Forces, causing considerable difficulties. On more than one occasion nearly ended my pursuit of becoming a Green Beret, in SFAS, the

SFQC and after, having made it to my first ODA. It wasn't that I was antisocial or unwilling to contribute to the success of the team, quite the contrary. Where problem resided was in believing striving for personal progress and development as focus would lead me to develop myself such I could go on and make greater contributions to the team. Turns out what I should have been doing the whole time was accepting there was no personal success unless it was team success, putting team ahead of my own growth and development. Even more difficult to understand and accept. Didn't matter I had a lot of successful life experience in more than one profession, I was new to this, without any practical experience. There was no way I could know how I needed to adjust my Vectors, to develop myself, in order I might best serve the mission and purpose of the team. Was a very long, at times painful, lesson to learn nothing we do is individual. There's no success for the individual but through the combined efforts of a team. If I could go back and tell my young self-anything. It would be, success is realized through complex webs of collaborative relationships. More precisely, working as an integral part of a team, putting the team before self.

Now I'm back in the private sector analyzing startup teams and leading my own high-functional team of highly qualified and experienced individuals. Find I owe a substantial debt to those many uncomfortable lessons earned during Special Forces Selection, the Q and years with my teammates on 14 after. Following, taken from these years and lessons, are five of the more personally painful and perhaps thereby, critical lessons from becoming and being a Green Beret, becoming a team player:

- *You're not who you think you are* – We've all sorts of ideas as to who we are, about our importance and place in the world. Reality, however, is most all of this, if attained in isolation, if untested in a high-functional team environment, is rubbish. Agree with their assessment or not, your team will tell you exactly who you are. This in how they interact with you, mostly indirectly. Rarely directly, though the best teams will be blunt and direct, particularly if you're young and still inexperienced or have transitioned to something new. While you need to stand for yourself and not be a weak pushover, allowing yourself to be maligned or bullied. You also need to shut up and listen because nine times out of ten, the team is right and you're not;

•   *The team's needs aren't your needs* – We can only better and improve ourselves, so we go on and make greater contributions to the many teams we're on. This means we must focus on personal and career development with careful and deliberate attention. But guess what. Our development and progress are never primary, only the development and progress of the team are. This means, while our career needs a certain thing to occur, if that isn't what the team needs at this time, it doesn't happen. This holds true regardless what position or authority you hold in the team. Only the team's needs matter.

•   *You have to let your team fail* – All teams fail. Even those few are 5-Vector Balanced high-functional teams with track records of incredible successes in firefights and RGBs. These failures happen due to externalities and internalities. Externalities being all the vast number of things change in the environment in which the team operates. Things can't be predicted or can't be mitigated away. Internalities most often being disagreement as to threats the team is facing, the Risk and Uncertainty Factors. Even if you see the RUF perfectly, even if you have the exact right answer. Doesn't mean the rest of the team will, though you must do everything you can to show them. This last, to a point only. Show them what you see, make alliances within the team, with leadership, seek to influence the team. But at that point where you realize the team has set its mind to something and there's no swaying them. Stop and let the team fail. Yourself included. If you can stop yourself at this point, let the team fail, it will recover and move on, having learned important lessons. Lessons can't be learned any other way. Keep pushing beyond this point and the discord you're introducing, rather than actual failure, will very likely destroy the team.

The hardest reality for most to live…

- *Your success isn't your own* – Stop taking credit for what you didn't do alone, for what wasn't fully developed in your mind. You may have had the original idea, but unless you brought it to the team fully formed in all its complexity, it doesn't belong to you. Conversely, if a teammate brought forward an idea you improved far more than the originator could, it doesn't belong to you either. Hard truth is, you most likely would never have come up with the idea or been able to develop it fully, were it not for the team. Ideas and their development into actionable and actioned plans don't spring out of nothing. Nor does their successful application occur only with the actions of one isolated and solitary teammate. That's simply not how the brain works, not how any of this works. Recognize those on your team for their contributions, direct and obvious and indirect and less-than-obvious, as a team and by name, and they'll recognize you in return.

And finally, leading directly from the above, the single most important of all…

- *There is only the team* – We're certainly inextricably hardwired, millions and millions of years of evolution, right down to the cellular level, for tribalism. For us versus them. This can lead to some of the worst of human behaviour. It does. But doesn't have to, nor does it mean all of this wiring for tribalism, for the team first, is bad or unhealthy. There is amazing power in putting the team first, loyalty to the team above all else. At least for high-functional teams with proper 5-Vector Balances, capable of shifting and adapting rapidly to their environment. Focus on the team over self, on the self as only integral part of the whole, on your efforts being to perfect yourself such you can better contribute to the whole. An astonishing thing will happen. You'll unlock and tap into ancient neuronal networks predate humans and our primate ancestors. Neuronal networks which when tapped into allow for powerful synchronization with your teammates, making incredible contributions and successes possible for each and all.

Before moving on to discuss groupthink, which many teams falsely and dangerously believe is this synchronicity. Will put forward one further critical lesson here. Your actual team extends far beyond your functional team, even beyond all the employees of your startup. It includes your vendors, partners and allies, investors and most critically of all, customers and clients. As example of why we need to really understand and accept this reality. I once, quite unintentionally, developed an adversarial relationship with our lead investor. Such he was forced to teach me a painful lesson I've never forgotten. Having made some foolish 'us-vs-them' statement, he told me bluntly, he and his firm were teammates, without whom we wouldn't succeed. A lesson I had to finally learn a few months later, through withdrawn financial supports leading to business failure, supports our investor would've extended had I not developed an adversarial relationship, had I taken into account the needs of all of our teammates, had I put the entire team first.

Groupthink Kills

"Embrace what you don't know, especially in the beginning, because what you don't know can become your greatest asset. It ensures that you will absolutely be doing things different from everybody else."

— Sara Blakely, SPANX founder

****

Born in a small village, during an era of Chinese occupation, orphaned as a toddler, you're raised by your elder brother. From a young age you defy tradition, choosing to be a warrior rather than someone's wife. You will convince men to follow you in battle, leading your own troops in rebellion against the Chinese. Over the years you will come to run the countryside, establishing your own military base, training a thousand rebels. When your brother attempts to dissuade  you, you famously state, "I will not resign myself to the lot of women who bow their heads and become concubines. I wish to ride the tempest, tame the waves, kill the sharks. I have no desire to take abuse."

Before age of 21 you'll have fought in over 30 successful battles against the Chinese with your own rebel army. Often riding an elephant into battle, your enemies will state, "It would be easier to fight a tiger than to face Lady Triệu in battle." In 248, after losing a decisive battle against the Chinese, rather than be taken hostage to be humiliated by men you had humiliated in battle for years. You commit suicide by drowning yourself in a river.

You're Triệu Thị Trinh (225-248AD), upon your death you'll become a symbol of courage and defiance, inspiring women and the people of Vietnam, to stand and fight rather than shamefully bow the neck. It's rumored you haunted the dreams of Vietnamese revolutionaries for centuries, providing guidance to the freedom fighters came after you. Even to this day, almost two millennia on, you're revered as a national hero in Vietnam. So that Westerners may understand your strength, courage and influence, despite you came centuries before her. You're known in the West as the Vietnamese Joan d'Arc, your story told around the world to this very day.

****

In the postmodernist world we've allowed to arise over the past century, Political Correctness forcing us ever more into the worst of tribalism, violent identity politics. Groupthink is becoming the norm. With emotion laden and driven mob rule replacing rational reality driven reason. Though it takes some amount of time to see the results of this groupthink in civilizations, invariably ending in tyranny and total collapse. Results are immediate and obvious when it comes to startups and SpecOps missions, both fail, destroying assets and even taking lives unnecessarily. On the many battlefields of war, startups and most certainly politics, groupthink kills. There's no more destructive force than everyone thinking the same way. Bending interpretations of information and intelligence to say what you want them to say, to support what you want to do rather than what needs to be done. Groupthink becomes orders of magnitude more deadly when built on incomplete information, information completely ignored, intentionally falsified, information of such complexity it's not so easy to understand or which was purpose modelled to your cognitive biases in a brilliantly indirect fashion by an enemy seeking your demise. All of which occurs even with rational reality driven thinking and decision-making but assuming deadly power when combined with the malevolence of mob rule.

Groupthink isn't only everyone thinking exact same thing or in the exact same way. Generally, subsets of a bigger group retreat into a particular camp, camps organized around small differences of opinion, interpretation, around little more than variations on a theme. These smaller groups, incapable of prevailing alone in a conflict, form alliance with other small groups. This is natural and when done right can lead to great stability and even be means by which to stave off groupthink. The problem arises from brain wiring which necessitates that if we retreat into a camp, into defensive or defense through offense thought. We inescapable begin skewing incoming information and interpretation to support our now fortified and defended position, to sustain our alliance and its stated grievances. Meaning once we've retreated into a camp and have formed alliances to defend our camp, we start to see everything in the context of us-vs-them, we're right and they are wrong, we're good and they are bad, we must win and they must lose. Much like the trenches of WWI, now we're organized into dug in and fortified defensive positions, these must always be manned and vehemently fought for. Doesn't matter the real enemy is an external threat to all. Groupthink ensure we always devolve into fighting among ourselves.

Groupthink in politics, business and general warfare, arises from only one or both of two starting conditions. The first is total adherence to an ideological and philosophical view of the world, to what you believe is and what you believe must happen. Regardless both may have virtually no or absolutely zero base in reality, being pure fabrication of the mind, yours or another. The second, arising from the first, though at times leading to, is surrounding yourself with people ideologically and philosophically filter the world the same or similarly to same cognitively biased way in which you do. Despite very likely having it all wrong, you surround yourself with those you believe are necessary to make happen what your biased mind believes necessary, shunning all with differing views.

Real danger arises from fact, one's ideology is constructed upon an infinitesimal fraction of available information, with this fraction of information heavily influenced by those who shaped the information according to their own ideological and philosophical leanings before feeding it to others. In our Postindustrial world, massive volumes of new information daily, increasingly capable information operations spreading brilliantly targeted disinformation. It's become impossible to know anything for certain fact, with those few certain facts do exist, virtually impossible to contextually value given the vastly increasing amount of new information. Information overload, and information warfare are driving most of us to resort to our built-in cognitive biases, simply to get through a day functionally. This's immeasurably dangerous given, once one's ideology and philosophy are set, 80% result of genetic predispositions and 20% to early environment. The brain itself, without any need for conscious thought, will go to any length to prevent cognitive dissonance, from having to process reality in any other way. This, no matter how valid or obvious actual reality is.

Even when confronted starkly, strikingly, with a reality that falls well outside tolerance of one's ideology and philosophy, in ways that cannot be refuted with even modest application of intelligence. It requires a massive shock over a prolonged period of time to force one to see the truth of it. Let us make no mistake. The brain is an incredible liar. It possesses the incredible ability to lie to itself at the neuronal level, at times fundamentally changing interpretation of sensory input not after but at point of experience, setting false information into memory. This so as to ensure adherence to early established patterns of belief and neural processing, information biasing. Doesn't matter who we are, how well developed and stable we are. Biasing of information is happening in all of us all the time. This means that if your team isn't balanced in the right way, groupthink will at some point rise and destroy it.

Right, we're screwed! Cognitive bias is built right into brain structures and processes. There's so much information and disinformation, even were we to try, we couldn't see the real world, make unbiased decisions on factual and contextually relevant information. Why even try? Why give a damn at all? Why not allow devolution into groupthink, to mob rule. At least we'll have a chance for something. Well, quite aside from fact all the long history of mankind has been this very thing, striving to rise above the violence and destruction of groupthink and its biased, emotion derived and fueled mob rule. Your success, that is, your team's success, is dependent almost solely on your ability individually and as a team to be better than all this. So what can we do if our brains are wired to bias input, lying to us, if we're nature driven to surround ourselves with those biased same as us, if we don't possess enough time in busy lives to pursue our own information sourcing, intelligence development and testing?

Zen Buddhism would be a good place to start. However, it's a decades long, if not a many lives long, pursuit to reach the unbiased mind of a Zen master. Who has the time for that? Even if they did, why would they be in business or SpecOps, even if granted opportunity to participate in the exciting and rewarding Unconventional Warfare of startups and SF. I've spent forty-five years studying Zen Buddhism and I'm still nowhere near becoming a master of any sort. Despite this, and cognizant of my own greatly reduced yet unobliterated biases, I've come to look for three factors if found in startup founding or leadership team, means we won't invest.

1- Leadership has surrounded themselves with like-minded individuals from only one side of any ideological, philosophical and resultant political divide, with individuals only put forward what they believe leadership wants to hear, providing that information and those interpretations support leadership's bias derived beliefs;

2- Teams may be 5-Vector balanced well and unlike the first allowing for dissent and difference of opinion, even embracing and welcoming it, but which lack socioeconomic, sociocultural, educational and experiential diversity among the team, required for dissenting ideas and interpretations to provide leadership with more than mere variations of its own dominate biased beliefs;

3- Those maintain all the right balances, not just along 5-Vectors, also in line with those in #2 above, but which also just get along. It's creepy when people just get along, makes you wonder what they're hiding, and they're usually hiding something, cleverly disguised groupthink often being what's hidden. But more importantly, there are all critical dissenting views and opinions can only come from conflict and combat, from Running Gun Battles and firefights in which people died horribly, okay, at least their ideas died horribly.

Founders who develop any of the teams above, inevitably and inescapably fall into groupthink and are thereby blinded, incapable of getting ahead of market trends, of recognizing threats in time to respond or at all, even after failure. How does that old saying go, you can't know what you don't know. Groupthink prevents us from knowing anything but what the mob decries. Alexandre Koyré perhaps describes dangers of groupthink best in his *Réflexions sur le Mensonge*, "[t]he mob believes everything it is told, provided only that it be repeated over and over. Provided too that its passions, hatreds, fears are catered to. Nor need one try to stay within the limits of plausibility: on the contrary, the grosser, the bigger, the cruder the lie, the more readily is it believed and followed. Nor is there any need to avoid contradictions: the mob never notices; needless to pretend to correlate what is said to some with what is said to others: each person or group believes only what he is told, not what anyone else is told; needless to strive for coherence: the mob has no memory;

needless to pretend to any truth: the mob is radically incapable of perceiving it: the mob can never comprehend that its own interests are what is at stake."

The mob can be incredibly powerful and successful. That is, for a time, until market, civilization, community, company, team or other, figures out how to control, subvert, or feed it such the mob implodes under its inconsistencies. Startup teams blinded by groupthink, driven by cognitive biased thinking shared among a majority, or strong minority are no different. Hot startups and their teams can often by much like a mob, with wild success in the early days or after crossing some adoption threshold. These are rarely long-lived, with both internal and external actors and forces figuring out how to control, subvert or influence to implosion. Hardest thing for startup founders and teams to fight, to prevent mob control, is enticing nature of mobs. Mobs provide belonging and perception of empowerment, which are both great for marketing campaigns and pushes. That is, mobs are fueled by cheap and easy emotions rather than costly and difficult deliberate thought, making mobs incredibly attractive, at least in the short-term. Problem chasing this model is mobs are notoriously fickle, their attention spans very short.

Sadly, primates are designed, neurocognitively, to follow the mob, to seek out and support groupthink, leading ultimately to self-destructive behaviour. That is excepting us reclusive types and the immensely rare Alpha, both naturally shying away from mobs. Let's not confuse us Reclusive types with Introverts. The latter often joins the mob, privately, provides supports and gains rewards secretly from the sidelines of the spectacle. Problem with Alpha and Reclusive aversion to mobs is it prevents them from benefitting from the positive benefits of tribalism, and that of organized and healthy mobs. This last a rarity, but a reality, think 80,000 sports fans all like a mob at an American Football game, rarely ever turning bad. This mostly because they're of limited duration. Mobs aren't bad by being a mob, nor is the tribalism wired into our brains drives us to create and be a part of mobs. In a few rare cases in all of human history, the mob was both right and the only answer. As only viable response to real tyranny, not that imagined garbage passes for today fed ceaselessly to us by Postmodernists. At times in smaller or lager measure to right a wrong. Sometimes, as only way to bring to the attention of those blinded by groupthink that there is an actual problem. Even less often, the mob is sometimes required to protect the few from the many or the powerful. One caveat. When mobs are the solution is only true where there's incredibly strong leadership, not blinded nor bound by groupthink, leadership can carefully direct or shut the mob down if necessary. Don't think for a moment the mob itself is anything but a force for destruction. That's its only power and purpose. Not that this destructive force need be used always, merely threat of is usually enough.

After four decades Zen practice and thirty years in business, finance and SF, with more than one failure in each and all. Yes, couple of these failures due to my own having joined in groupthink, most however due to my having failed to benefit from the positive capacities of mobs. I've come to embrace the fact my processing at the neural level, influenced by my experiences, doesn't always allow me to see the truth, to overcome my own cognitive biases. Cognitive biases I've worked incredibly diligently to recognize and overcome. It is simply impossible for me to see or know anything in its fully truth, making it hard to see underlying shifts in the domains I work and invest in. In this same time, I've come to accept surrounding myself with those I like and only those driven by similar ideological and philosophical end goals, is the surest way to ultimately fail. To ensure none of the teams I'm involved with fall into this trap, I adhere to the following:

1. *I don't need to like you. I need to respect you* – The team needs contain members who're highly skilled, capable, experienced and connected in their domain, but who're also wired and conditioned by experiences and connections such they see the world differently than at least the final decision maker(s), even if what they see is dramatically different, causing conflict and combat, kicking off firefights, even if it means we don't all go out for drinks and have our kids play together in Zakynthos on holiday;

2. *I need be calm, quiet and genuinely listen* – While we might have exact right answer to exact right problem at exact right time. Doesn't mean we know what's really going on. Always be open and listen to everyone, at all times, even those unlikeable, those in lowly positions. Even when this leads to a firefight or another RGB. Regardless educational, professional, socioeconomic or sociocultural backgrounds, every human is empowered by an incredibly sophisticated brain, further empowered by unique life experiences gives them a perspective no other human has. At times the very perspective is only one capable of seeing and recognizing a problem or change in a market or organization;

3. *I am always student, never master* – Never fully trust yourself, your trained filters, or your carefully developed ability to interpret information and conduct what you believe to be neutral analysis of resulting intelligence. Always seek experience qualified advice, always bounce ideas off those whose judgement in that domain or along that avenue of reasoning is proven. Seek out those better than you, and there always are in any given domain, ask and learn And where possible, seek to do so with those who fundamentally see the world different than you, even if they're your enemy.

Malevolence

"Genuine tragedies in the world are not conflicts between right and wrong. They are conflicts between two rights"

— Georg Wilhelm Friedrich Hegel, Philosopher

****

Born during the first years of the 20th Century, in Khomein, Iran, raised by your aunt's family after your father's death and mother's relocation. You begin religious studies at Qom Seminary, age 16, becoming in time a leading Iranian Shiite scholar. 1941, you publish *Unveiling the Mysteries*, in which you lay out your argument for an Islamic government, believing the  laws of secular governments to be invalid as they don't arise from Allah. 1962, you're awarded title of Grand Ayatollah, one of only six. For your supports of increasingly radical and violent activism, you'll be expelled. From exile in 1970, you publish *Islamic Government: Governance of the Jurist*, outlining your own modern interpretation of the 9th Century Shiite concept of *vilayet-e faqih* (Guardianship of the Islamic Jurist). You modify this ancient concept, which shared powers, to one where a single cleric oversees all religious, military and governmental sectors, in order to ensure strict compliance with your interpretation of divine law.

From exile you'll foment rebellion and revolution back home in Iran. Conducting Unconventional Warfare within Iran, across the Middle East and around the world. Ensuring your concepts are enshrined in Iran's new constitution. Subverting military, legal, academic and many other Iranian organizations, elements and individuals from their loyalty to the state to loyalty to you. Upon your return, you'll unleash and support terrorism all across Iran. With your Islamic Revolutionary Guard Corp, you unleash hell on the Iranian people. Killing and terrorizing into submission any and all stand against or pose a threat to the idea of an Islamic State, and your power. Relying on violently malevolent terrorism, rather than the rightness of your purpose and cause, to take and hold power. Malevolent terrorism, you'll export globally. Destabilizing not only the entire Middle East, but eventually the entire world.

You're Ruhollah Khomeini (1900?–1989), in your desire to drag the world back to 9th Century beliefs and organizations of power, you'll unleash a reign of political assassinations, ruthless guerilla warfare and terrorism, has only grown stronger since your death. Tehran's support for militant groups continues, such as Hezbollah and Hamas, the Houthi and many others around the world. Iranian leaders using and exploiting these entities and their own fights, for power projection, undermining enemies at the same time helping like-minded groups. Integrating covert global insurgent warfare, in concert with open political mobilization, and every other means of total warfare. Using malevolence fueled terrorism and resultant fear, to dominate as much of the world as your successors are capable of. Tens of thousands killed every year, millions more displaced, homes, livelihoods and lives ruined. All to bring about your vision of a global Caliphate, dragging humanity back more than a thousand years into darkness and tyranny.

* *

First forty plus years, I put as little thought into malevolence as possible. Wanting to believe it immense rarity. Not being possessive of it myself. This fluke of nature over nurture, as I spent first fourteen years of my life living every single day with ever present, ever oppressive and violent malevolence. This from mother long before broken by her own malevolent mother. Didn't put much time and effort into thinking about malevolence, wishing to believe instead it not such a part of the human experience. Something could be meditated away if did exist. Two illusions I could believe in from insulated comfort of my first world life and from isolative life comes with being reclusive by nature. By time I'd gone on to pursue an early midlife crisis in joining Special Forces, I'd come to reluctantly accept both the undeniability and unavoidability of malevolence as a natural force. Resident in and powering more of our fellows than we will admit to in Judeo-Christian west, even less in the age of the great Disney Blank Slate lie.

In the yet Judeo-Christian west more dominantly, really in every first world community. First world being an economic definition related to level of development, no longer related to defined geographies. In these communities, the far greater percentage of citizens are insulated from the harsh realities of humanity. Citizens being kept secure and reality blinded in a protected bubble. Secured by those incredibly few go out and risk their lives daily to keep us safe, individuals see the world exactly as is. Individuals whose sole purpose is almost singularly to confront malevolence in its multifarious manifestations. Confronting often, very most extreme forms, forms it would be right to name evil. Though not the evil of some illusionary figures in a heaven and hell, but of humans right here among us. Why do we put a small percentage of our own our there, in harm's way, then vilify them for doing what they must to keep us safe?

We do it so we don't have to put ourselves at risk confronting evil, don't have to admit to darkness yet lies within the hearts and minds of man the animal. We do it so we won't have to give up our cherished comforts in order to provide more than platitudes, do something direct and personal of real meaning and value to humanity. We do it because everything is so complex it requires solid teams to address anything, good or bad, right or wrong, light or dark. And we're not so good at doing anything as teams anymore, outside being a mob. I've come to believe firmly we do it mostly though, because we don't want to admit we ourselves have some malevolence in us, oft used to personal benefit. This is however, a book on teamwork and on being a better team player, not the human condition. As such, will confine conversation herein on the role of malevolence to this context and not discuss what your law enforcement and Special Operations Forces, though not only these, live with and confront every day out there, out at and beyond the very protected bubble allows for startups, teams, teamwork and leadership. If you want a more detailed image of malevolence in our modern world, take a read of my upcoming novel, *As Rome Burns*.

Last three years on an ODA, I served as Assistant Operations and Intelligence Sergeant for our team and troop, conducting a very specific mission within the far larger counterterrorism and counterproliferation mission. Usually working sixteen or more hours a day, six days a week. Such was the scope of the threat, and this not in any combat theatre but well outside the theatres of Iraq and Afghanistan. Most of my time was spent looking through vast amounts of information from a broad array of sources and types, looking for the ever so faint threads identified presence of malevolent intent and activity. Not looking at terrorists, foot soldiers of the global terrorist insurgency, but at the many facilitators: bankers, investors, shipping and logistics companies, charitable organizations, finance networks, and general every day run of the mill life in the parts of the world we were forced to target. The sheer scope of those involved in malevolent activities around the world is stunning. This with malevolence a spectrum from tacit agreement from the sidelines up through all the many ways in which malevolent activity is directly and indirectly supported right up to the actual act of murder. This including far more than just terrorist organizations.

The last four years, conducting doctoral studies, particularly two years focused on sentiment analysis and Hidden Markov

Chains, trying to ensure behavioural modeling AI recognizes faint gossamer whispers of malevolence. Kept running up against the undeniable ghosted signature of malevolence in information flows. Everyday information flows had nothing to do with terrorism or what most would consider malevolent intent and activity. Malevolence is everywhere. Something we live with every single day. Most of it going unrecognized, often even by those employing it. In most of its applications, malevolence is subtle, hard to trace and quite despite the unbelievable number of variations in its expression, seems to arise from only one single root, Envy. The inevitable and inescapable product of the zero-sum mindset. While the end expression of envy born malevolence is literarily impossible to map, malevolence itself breaks into two primary forms.

-   *Human Malevolence* | Most brains on this planet are wired for scarcity, hardwired belief there's a limited amount of resources. Scarcity wiring prevalent in the 96% of humans aren't Alphas or Sigmoids, represents itself behaviourally as Envy. Envy wired into our self-valuation and motivation and reward circuits, ensures the brain effortlessly justifies taking, justification necessary in order the individual conducting the malevolent act of taking, isn't driven to cognitive dissonance.

Malevolence isn't a thing. But rather a thought process and resultant action. Thought process makes you believe you've less and therefore justified in taking. Followed by the action of taking what isn't yours to take. Specifically, taking what isn't yours to take for express purpose to reduce another or others. This taking takes many forms. From the very small, such as the snide word placed such it reduces someone's psychological balance or stature in the eyes of others to slander and libel designed to ruin someone's career and personal standing. To theft of property and freedoms, from something as small as taking someone's pencil to taking their purse, from valuables in their home to funds in their accounts, from kidnapping and extortion to the taking of freedoms ranging from personal time to forced adherence to oppressive rules, laws and regulations to outright slavery. Only in the very extreme is malevolent taking in the form of taking someone's life. This mostly as there's little profit in it and it comes with high costs, that's except in cases where profit is sufficient, costs marginal enough, to warrant murder or even genocide.

While not a scientific backed set of numbers, my experience and readings of a substantial body of studies and literature, lead me to live with the following set of assumptions when it comes to malevolence, its application and resultant taking:

- 1% | Purely malevolent individuals with zero of the internal control mechanisms prevent resorting to violence as first course of action;

- 10% | Purely malevolent individuals with some of the control mechanisms but which have zero problem resorting to violence if the situation allows;

- 30% | Including both the above, those who're purely malevolent but which only resort to violence if they believe they can get away with it;

- 50% | Those not purely malevolent, who won't resort to violence, but do employ malevolent taking to the degree they believe they can get away with it;

- 16% | Those not purely malevolent, who recognize envy within themselves and who work diligently to remove or otherwise manage it such it can't manifest as malevolence;

- 4% | 1% Alphas, 3% Sigmoids, Sigmoids being yet unrealized Alphas, neither possess envy or malevolence and by nature of psychological makeup, actively resist through influence and directly fight against malevolence in the many teams they're part of, responsible for.

- *System Malevolence* | Systems are established for the purpose of optimizing finite resources. This means they are zero-sum by design. To maximize this optimization, skilled managers are required, zero-sum thinkers, who thoroughly know the bounded limitations of the system, finite resources and all the many intricate internal and external dependencies. Zero-sum minded employees are required in large numbers, those need structured systems, bounded by known rules and behavioural constraints that limit pure competition and all out warfare, structure allowing the noncompetitive to feel safe and secure, to be artificially competitive.

It's not that systems are purpose established to be malevolent, most are in fact established for express purpose of resisting or otherwise mitigating malevolent activity within a given community or communities. In the case of business systems, to maximize resource utilization such a far greater number of the community benefits from innovations and has access to necessary items at affordable price points and of sufficient quality. Systems inevitably become malevolent however, at the point where they begin to have internal processes, rules and practices consume 50% or more of the productivity of employees and managers. These systems become attractive at this point to those who're driven by malevolent intent. This as the system itself begins to turn inwards, becoming increasingly divorced from the need to innovate, isolated from reality, managers and employees becoming ever more insulated from paying price for their actions. This doesn't only occur in large systems, but in virtually any organization, formal entity, group, division, working group or team. The worst occurs in systems possessing forms of enforcement power, producing little or nothing outside the application of this enforcement. Systems which must become ever more oppressive as they develop ever more rules in order to ensure the power to enforce.

Agencies of governments and world organizations and lending institutions being worst offenders. With most arms of such in time becoming little more than purpose designed, led and managed for malevolent taking. Most often this slide into tyranny not intentioned but arising from necessity to optimize. That's, till leadership, senior management and employee positions become populated mostly by those who are malevolence motivated, using the power of the system to carry out their taking unhindered, protected and sheltered within a now impersonal system of complex rules, policies and procedures, with ever less accountability at the level of the individual, even less at level of the system.

We'll never be able to remove zero-sum brain wiring, move beyond Envy driving the single most powerful force in all human existence, malevolence. We'll never be able to devise systems make malevolent action impossible. And perhaps we shouldn't try. Evolution has had hundreds of millions, billions, of years to work out optimal solutions. We can't say with confidence malevolence to such a degree isn't critically important to our survival and progress. If it wasn't, nature would have bred it out of the gene pool long ago. This truth doesn't mean we shouldn't be aware of it, shouldn't push back against it, shouldn't seek to root it out within ourselves and develop ourselves such malevolence is not our dominate tool to rely upon to progress through life.

Seems to me the purpose of a life should be this very thing, pushing back against malevolence, in self, in our teams and organizations and in all of humanity. This requires being an incredibly solid team player. Being invited and contributing maximally to high-functional teams. Not pursuing happiness but rising to greater and greater levels of capacity such our teams, organizations and communities are more resilient and better protected from malevolence will inevitably arise both from within and without. This means knowing our own 5-Vector Balance at any given moment, how it's determined by our malevolence and our response to the malevolence of others, personal and impersonal alike. This same required of our team as a whole and across all the many teams we're contributors to.

Summary

"I slept and dreamed that life was joy. I woke and I saw that life is all service. I served and I saw that service was joy."
— Rabindranath Tagore, Poet

****

We've a lot of work yet to be done as we transition and move deeper into the 21st Century, evolving beyond an Industrial to a Postindustrial economic base. And with some struggles yet ahead, shedding the structural malevolence of the Postmodernist world assembled over the past two centuries. It's not going to be easy. As evidenced looking around us at rising levels of uncertainty, conflict, strife and Unconventional Warfare in every corner and virtually every community on the planet. This as all those systems, structures and their managers and employees whose power, position and incomes are built on the old, fight with all in their capacity to retain the increasingly malevolent world they understand and know well how to operate within, to optimize. This is work we must all be about, work can't be done alone, by a few or in isolation. This work forces us to be highly contributory members of high-functional teams. Not only a single team, but many teams, teams will change over time driven by current and emerging situational requirements and needs. We also won't just fill one specific highly refined role for all the years of our professional lives, but several or many, requiring our own constant evolution.

One cannot evolve and keep up with the pace of change, unless one truly knows self, not as a static thing with clear transitions between states of being. But as an ever-changing thing, as something changes constantly, these changes driven by internal and external forces concurrently. To successfully participate in the ultra-high-paced, high-Risk and Uncertainty now globalized, Postindustrial economy, as member of high-functional teams. Requires we know at any moment our own 5-Vector Balance and that of our team. More, we need know how to best utilize our own 5-Vector Balance and that of our team, such we as self and we as a team, prevail in the many firefights our professional and personal lives are really constructed of. So, strap on your preferred sidearm, link up with your ODA, and set to the work of the many Running Gun Battles required of success in this time of massive change!

Image Sources:

1. AeroArt International; Khutulun, Mongol Princess Warrior w/Snow Leopard; Source: http://www.aeroartinc.com/khutulun-mongol-princess-warrior-w-snow-leopard.html
2. Gelatin silver print of William Harvey Carney; 1901-1908; Source: Moorland-Spingam Research Center, Howard University; Author: James Reed – Public Domain
3. Musashi Miyamoto with two Bokken (wooden quarterstaves) Color version to replace B&W. Scan of ancient Japanese scroll – Public Domain
4. Lozen; WikiTree; Original digital image: 320 x 428 pixels. Google software. – Public Domain
5. Portrait of Maratha prince Shivaji with a detailed Dutch caption on the decorated frame – Public Domain
6. The detail of the Alexander Mosaic showing Alexander the Great – Public Domain
7. Grace O'Malley the Pirate Queen, History in Co. Mayo; Source: http://www.mayo-ireland.ie/en/about-mayo/history/grace-omalley-the-pirate-queen.html
8. Xiahou Dun Portrait – Public Domain
9. Triệu Thị Trinh – Public Domain
10. Ruhollah Khomeini – Public Domain

ABOUT THE AUTHOR

E.M. Burlingame, author of Starving for Leadership and As Rome Burns, is Founder – Honos Foundation, fostering entrepreneurship and investment in conflict repressed communities and Founder – Emerio Group, a technology developer and early-stage investment firm. He studied Strategic Studies and Defense Analysis with emphasis on Special Operations and economics at Norwich and is completing his Doctoral studies in Interdisciplinary Engineering, with emphasis on Computational Engineering at UAB. He's served with both 1st and 20th Special Forces groups and worked in investment banking, private equity and venture capital. Having also co-founded and founded his own technology startups.

www.ingramcontent.com/pod-product-compliance
Lightning Source LLC
Chambersburg PA
CBHW070604220526
45467CB00003B/1297